Many Runaway Horses

Stories of *Almost* Dying Horseback

By Alex Tyson

For My mom, who let me ride horses.
She first gave me life, and then gave it again by giving up
everything so I could ride.

About this Book

One of the greatest gifts my mother was able to give me was the ability to ride horses. We could only afford one lesson a week and could barely afford board and horse shows. My mom used all of her tip money from her job as a hair dresser to pay for my horse habit.

I was the classic barn rat, I lived at the barn. I was there almost every day as soon as school got out and every weekend. I took on non-paying jobs just to have an excuse to be there more. I became the catch rider at the barn I grew up at, riding all sorts of horses: Quarter Horses, Morgans, Thoroughbreds, Warmbloods, Friesians, Arabians, Percherons, Clydesdales, Paso Finos, Tennessee Walkers, Halflingers, Welsh Ponies, and every type of mixed grade horse. I rode the barn owner's horses, my trainer's horses, boarders' horses, any horse anyone would let me climb aboard.

I had the good fortune to be around all disciplines, and cross trained in hunter/jumper, western pleasure, dressage, barrel racing, trail riding, and natural horsemanship.

Naturally, living at the barn and getting to ride all sorts of horses all day leaves lots of opportunities for shenanigans. This book is an attempt to document some of the zanier things that happened to me. As the saying goes, "Wisdom comes from experience, and experience comes from bad judgment."

Many of these adventures could have resulted in a newspaper article recounting my death rather than a funny story to tell later. I have attempted to describe each event from my point of view at the time, what I was feeling and what I was thinking. At the end of most stories, I have included some insights as an adult and also now as a horseback riding instructor. Some of the stories are just funny, some are great moments I experienced and were not so much what I did wrong, but what I did right.

Some names and identifying details have been changed and some timelines moved around, but these are my stories. I tell these stories to my riding students all the time, as cautionary tales, and maybe a little bit of bragging. I fully realize to some people these are insane stories and to others this is their typical Sunday ride. I am not to be seen as the most outlandish, craziest rider out there—if anything, I'm hoping to bring awareness to the fact that many near disasters can be avoided with a little planning and common sense. Just because you can do it, doesn't mean you should.

Not all the stories describe near-death experiences, but all were the result of a mostly unsupervised, horse-crazy kid let loose with her friends in the early 2000s. With today's "nanny" mentality, cell phones, video surveillance, and far more parent involvement that I could ever fathom as a kid, horse kids now will most likely still get themselves into trouble, but the flavor will be a little different.

I hope you enjoy reading about them as much I as enjoyed living them. Well, I enjoy talking about them now-at the time, most were terrifying.

Many Runaway Horses

First Fall

It's been said if you haven't fallen, you're not really riding. Well, my first fall really "set the bar high." I was nine years old and the horse was a 17.2hand-high (about five foot eight inches at the horse's shoulder) grey Percheron named "Tiny." This fall set the tone for my riding life moving forward: dramatic.

At the time, I was taking lessons at Haverhill Farms, the largest riding school in Michigan for many years. The facility, which had about fifty school horses and two indoor arenas, was a hunter-jumper facility, so I was in an English style saddle (designed to jump, an English saddle is pretty minimal—you keep your seat primarily using your legs and your balance) on top of this giant beast of a horse.

There were jumps set up just inside the outer track of the arena on the quarter-line. I had been cantering for a few months but I had yet to canter without stirrups, which was the school's criteria for learning how to jump. This was my dream: I had seen show jumping on TV and I wanted to wear that red coat and sail over those high jumps in front of a packed stadium. I could see that in my mind's eye, I could be brave, I could fly, and everyone would think I was such an awesome rider in that red coat. That is all I wanted to be in my whole life, a GOOD rider.

I saw all those things in my mind, but I was still learning to canter. "Why not?" I thought, you have to dream big if anything good is going to happen to you. All the people who have made anything happen say so.

I had all these goals and aspirations, but I was a good student who always did EXACTLY as she was told; I never bucked the system or tried to get around it. I knew there was a system, an order to learning how to ride and I subscribed to it, even if I didn't fully understand it. You had to steer the horse, then trot, then posting trot, sitting trot, two-point, trot without stirrups, go over ground poles, canter without stirrups, then jumping.

So, as I was cantering along the ring and passing one of my classmates on the quarter line, I had no thoughts whatsoever about going over the jump that was in the distance in front of me. I was just going to go around the jump to the inside and then back on the rail, or main path by the wall, at the corner.

But Tiny, as horses often do, had other ideas. She seemed to lock onto the jump, ears forward, head up, body a little tense. I knew I was getting close to the jump, and didn't want to hit it so I pulled my inside rein, closed my outside leg, looked to my path forward towards the center of the arena, and asked her to steer around the jump.

Nothing.

I shortened my reins by putting them both quickly in my right hand and sliding my left down towards the bit. I braced, pulling that rein sideways and upwards trying to get Tiny's head and neck facing away from the jump, all the while kicking with my outside leg, encouraging her to move over. All of these efforts were in vain and I knew we were going to hit it; we couldn't be more than three strides away at this point.

"Two-point!" my instructor shrieked as I got closer to the fence.

I did what she said and got into the two-point or jumping position. It had not occurred to me that Tiny might jump the fence, I just thought we were going to crash into it. Now, we can jump it, maybe.

If I hold on enough, I can hopefully stay on as this big beast lumbers over this fence. I reached my hands a third of the way up her neck, and grabbed her mane in a death grip, tangling it around my little fingers. I got my body hinged forward at the hips, up out of the saddle and sank all my weight into my heels to try and stay balanced.

I was ready.

I braced for the leap upward but it didn't come. At the last moment, Tiny decided not to jump the fence, but instead ducked out to the left. I didn't realize what she did, but I did realize that I was falling. Tiny wasn't over me but running away from the jump. I flew sideways into the standard holding up the jump poles, my shoulder hitting it first, thankfully missing my head, and then my whole body rotated and spun as I hit it.

Upon impact, the jump standard fell down, taking all of the poles with it, scattering about. I heard a loud gasp come from my instructor and the other kids in the class. I heard the teacher yell for everyone to stop their horses. When I went to get up off my side the teacher was right there next to me, stopping my movement while she fired off questions,

"Are you ok?"

"Does your head hurt?"

"How about your legs... your side?"

"Do you see any stars?"

We did an inventory on all of my body parts and concluded that I was, indeed, ok and that I was ok to get back on. I knew I had to get back on, and I wasn't going to fight anyone on it, but I didn't want to canter again. As if almost reading my mind, the instructor said,

"You do have to get on and walk around, but there isn't time to canter again so you don't have to do that."

Whew!

I shakily got back on Tiny, who seemed unfazed by the encounter, and walked around the arena for the five minutes that remained in the lesson. Nothing more was directly said to me other than, "that was quite the fall." When I informed people that it was my first one, they were utterly shocked. I think they were more shocked that I wasn't crying. I was mostly shocked by the damage I had done to the jump. The standard and five or so poles were splattered all over the ground. It was a mess, a mess I created.

When I got off and went to put Tiny away, I realized that between my thighs there was a large blood-stained cut on my breeches. The fabric was torn away in decently clean line, curving up from the back of my thigh toward the center of my leg. The cut underneath wasn't too deep, but there was a fair amount of blood everywhere. It had even seeped a bit into the leather of the saddle. After I was done untacking, I went back up to the instructor and showed her my discovery. Her eyes got as big as dinner plates as she thought about what could have happened.

"Let's go over to the jump and look to see what it was…does it hurt?" she asked.

"Nope." I said with a sheepish smile. I was just a little shocked that my sport had drawn blood.

We walked over to the jump, still strewn about the arena and the instructor carefully examined the poles, the standard, and the flower boxes. There were no wood splinters anywhere so it didn't look like I was cut by that. I had been completely ejected from the saddle so it wasn't anything to do with getting hung up on any tack. A hoof wouldn't have made a mark like this from being stepped on.

"Ah-ha!" she exclaimed! And crouched down to the fallen standard to point at the only metal thing in sight: a jump cup. A jump cup is a curved piece of metal (or later plastic for this very reason) that is secured to the jump standard with a pin, and holds the poles in place on the jump.

"When you hit the jump and then twisted around, I bet you cut your leg on this!" I looked at it and just raised my eye brows at her, not really sure what to say.

"That was quite a fall! Just wash the cut with soap and water, you will be ok."

I left that day with an odd sense of pride at having survived my first fall, more still that it seemed to be cooler than other people's "firsts." Someone also informed me as I was leaving that I was "In the club" now, and that I "have to fall seven times before you are a real rider... six more to go!" When I had first started riding at Haverhill, I remember the man who gave us our paperwork, an elderly gentleman, had looked me dead in the eye as my mom was signing the release of liability forms and said,

"You could die doing this you know... at any time you could die. Are you ok with that?" he asked as he looked right through my soul. I nodded my head pretty definitely for a young kid.

"Are you?" he asked my mom.

"Well, uh, yeah, we are here" my mom said back. At the time that seemed to satisfy him, and we proceeded forward.

Now, a year or so later, I understood more of what he meant by that statement. I was doing a dangerous thing; a thing that people are afraid of. But I was okay, falling wasn't that bad, and I got back on. Next week I would do it again. I was in the club; I was a horseback rider. I felt pretty accomplished and oddly at peace with the fall, but I still didn't tell Mom anything about what happened. In fact, I made a point to play around in my breeches and get them all muddy so she would think that is how I ripped them. I was okay, she didn't need to know more.

~Adult Reflections~

As riding instructor, I would always communicate that the student fell to the adult in charge of the child. I would also explain concussion symptoms and what to look for. Falls are inevitable in horseback riding. It is not if, but when and how bad you fall.

That being said, it is our duty as horse professionals to do whatever we can to minimize or eliminate preventable falls. In retrospect, my experience fell into a grey area. On the one hand, a too powerful horse, too little kid, a jump in the arena and not enough skill was a risky situation. On the other, perhaps my riding instructor really did think I could handle it, but then, well... I didn't. Sometimes you have to take risks to see how it works out.

Unfortunately, I can't recall my instructor's name or face, so I can't ask her about it now. In either case, I will always be thankful that she told me the best thing possible to do in that situation, and checked on me afterwards. The whole thing gave me more respect for what I was doing, and I got major street credit from taking such a fall!

Not Tiny, but school horse Collete and I at Haverhill around the same time.

Alex Tyson

Pepper

    Things can change so quickly and serendipitously. For my first horse, I have my mother to thank. My mom is the definition of whimsical; she is spontaneous, and only has one foot on the ground. It's gotten her into a lot of trouble over the years, and this was no different. A horse is the definition of trouble: vet bills, feed bills, tack, lessons, board, training, shows! As they say, it ain't the horse, it's the "stuff!"

    It started innocently enough. There was a 4-H meeting being held in Ortonville, the next town over from where we lived in Holly. My mom thought it would be a good idea if we attended. I didn't know much about 4-H, but being horse crazy and always looking for another opportunity to ride, I was happy to go.

    At the meeting, I sat next to two girls my age named April and Liz. April lived on a small horse farm not far from the community building where we were at, and Liz boarded her horse there. All being horse crazy, we hit it off right away. As soon as the meeting started, I knew that this 4-H thing would be hard for me. I rode once a week at Haverhill and went to horse camp in the summer, but that is all that we could afford. I had asked my mom for a horse hundreds of times but the answer was always no. Horses are too expensive. We can't afford it. I had asked so many times I knew not to ask again. I would leave the meeting with new friends, but I really wouldn't be able to do 4-H.

    Unbeknownst to me my mom was sitting with Tracy, April's mom, who told Mom all about her farm, which wasn't far from here, and about a horse that one of her boarders had for sale. Tracy told her the price of the horse, the board, what it included, and by the end of the meeting my mom had it all figured out.

When Mom came to gather me, she had a glint in her eye, a hint of mischief.

"Well, if you are going to do this, you are going to need a horse!" she declared, as if by this self-evident fact we were going to get one.

"Yeah, I think so..." I said. What was she up to?

"Well," she continued, "I just met Tracy here, and it looks like you are now friends with her daughter April," she gave a coy little smile in April's direction before turning back to me. "And...well...there is this horse for sale at their farm for $500."

My eyes got as big as saucers and I started jumping up and down,

"And, we are going to go look at it Saturday!"

"WHAT!" I shrieked! "YES,YES,YES,YES,YES, THANK YOU!!!" I screamed and ran up to my mom and gave her a huge bear hug.

Good things do happen. I was going to get to have my dream life. I was going to have a horse!!

"Now, we have to be sure it will be a good fit," Tracy interjected, bringing a little bit of reality into the situation, but not enough to dissuade eleven-year-old me from my excitement. "But if it works out, you can board at our place."

A new horse. New friends. I could be the kind of person who owns a horse! I could ride every day! April, Liz, and I could be like our very own saddle club! I can't believe it. My life is going to change. This is everything my heart has ever wanted. A horse to call my own, and friends who understand me and like horses too.

The meeting was Thursday, so I only had to wait two more days to meet my new horse, Pepper was her name. She was a twenty-year-old flea bitten gray, and, according to

Tracy, half Arabian. I loved *The Black Stallion* books! I would have an Arabian! How exotic!

Mom, naturally, didn't tell my dad of her plans to buy me a horse. She did, however, go over every detail of the expense with me. In 2003 prices, this was:
Cost of horse: $500
Cost of board: $100 per month
Cost of shavings: $3 a bag, 2-3 bags per week
Cost of grain: approximately 1-2 bags a month, $13 a bag for Purina senior
Hay: 1 bale a week at $2 a bale

The deal with this type of board was that it was almost all self-care. Tracy would feed and let the horses out of their stalls in the morning, but we were responsible for cleaning stalls. Stalls needed to be cleaned at least every other day. We had to provide the hay and the grain for the horse separately, but she would feed.

"Now, you are going to have to clean Pepper's stall…I know how much you hate cleaning!"

"No, Mom, it won't matter… It's cleaning a *horse's stall* not my room!" This seemed rather obvious to me.
Mom chuckled because she knew it was true.

At the time my mom had a gold Chevy Malibu-not what one would typically transport hay and grain with. Not to be dissuaded, in the two days between the 4-H meeting to the horse meet-and-greet, Mom had found a local hay guy willing to sell her one bale a week, and put it in the trunk of her car. She also found a Tractor Supply Company store that was more or less on her way home from work, and she got the shavings and the grain there. She figured that the total cost of the horse would be under $150 a month, and that she could manage that, and that her car could transport all that we needed for one horse.

"I think the guy that sold me the hay thinks I am crazy," she told me.

"Look at this crazy lady putting a bale of hay in the trunk of her car! Oh well, we do what we have to do. Even if it isn't normal, we do it." She said this with her head held high, proud that she figured out how to get her daughter a horse. Mind you we hadn't gotten the horse yet, but she was ready and proud all the same.

It is worth mentioning that naive, eleven-year-old me knew with absolute certainty the fickleness of the situation and how delicately it must be handled. My mom had agreed to *this horse* and *this situation.* An identical situation, even at the same cost would most likely not do. She liked the people, it was close by, and she thought she could afford it. If I was to get a horse, I knew that it had to be *this horse.* My future as a horse owner relied on this deal going through. It *had* to work. Pepper needed to be my horse, whether I liked her or not.

As Saturday came, I had all the feelings. My chest was tight, I was breathing quickly, I had ALL the butterflies in my stomach, all at once, flapping around in there with unbridled joy, ready to burst forth from my throat and dance around in front of me. I could hardly contain it.

This is really happening I told myself over and over, *this is happening, you are going to get a horse!*

Pepper was tied up to a fence and looked our direction as we approached the barn.

She looked at me! She is interested in me! She wants me to be her new owner!

As I walked towards her, I am sure that I skipped across the ground slightly as I tried to keep my jitters in check. The world was opening up and full of wonderful colors, hopes, and possibilities. The sun was brighter, and the grey horse shone in the morning light. Anything could happen. Corie, Pepper's owner, explained that this was her childhood horse and that she had outgrown her. Corie, who had clearly moved on from childhood whimsies into a tight tank top and a push up bra, was looking at getting an off the track thoroughbred, or OTTB, to further her riding skills and it was time for Pepper to find a new home with another little girl. She really emphasized that part, she wanted Pepper to go to a kid. I felt a little animosity to Corie. She was leaving her horse! I could protect her; I could love her. Why do adults get rid of things they don't want any more? How unfair to Pepper!

Of course, I didn't say any of this and just stood and stroked Pepper while the adults talked. I didn't need to say anything, I was with my horse. Eventually, they stopped talking and got Pepper's tack. I didn't have any of this equipment, so when Corie went to get her own tack, my mom realized she would have to spend more money on riding equipment. I could tell she was a little concerned, and asked Tracy and Corie what some tack might cost,

"Maybe $200-300 for everything if you get it used." Corie said to her.

Mom looked a little concerned, but picked her chin up and looked at me getting ready, tacking Pepper up. Smiling she squeaked out, "ok... ok" with a nervous headshake.

Luckily for me, I had learned to ride at Haverhill. I was used to essentially riding a different horse every time I rode. Tall, short, narrow, wide, slow, speedy, and every combination thereof, I could get on and adjust pretty quickly. I could canter pretty well and ride without stirrups, so I wasn't worried about getting on Pepper and being able to ride her. I knew I would be fine.

Tracy had a dirt arena, with electric fence for the border. I knew the shock I would get if I was careless and was careful not to get too close. I walked Pepper around, trotted both directions and everything was going pretty well. When I asked her to canter, Pepper started out at a nice gait but then quickly sped up into the fastest canter I had ridden to date. I knew enough to remain calm and try to stay in control but I wasn't able to slow her down.

Don't panic. Don't look like you are scared or you will never get a horse. Figure it out, you have to ride this horse. It has to be this horse. This is your horse.

Eventually I did get her to go back down into a trot and I pulled her up alongside Corie and my mom. "She went a little fast, didn't she?" Mom asked, a little worried, but also unsure of what she was seeing.

"Oh, I know," I replied, "I asked her to do that, I wanted to see how much speed she had." I lied.

I didn't look over at Corie, but she didn't offer any advice and didn't say anything to rat me out. I am sure she could tell I wanted the horse, plus, she wanted to sell the horse. I just walked Pepper around after that, I wasn't sure what to do, and I was a little scared. I wanted a horse so, so, so bad, but this horse was a bit more that I could handle.

This is what my riding instructors meant when they told someone, "This horse is too much for you, she needs an advanced rider." Pepper clearly needed a more advanced rider to control her. This was my only path to horse ownership, so I would have to become an advanced rider. I also couldn't let my mom know how scared I was because then she wouldn't go through with it.

I needed to put on an excited face and move forward. This was my horse; I was going to figure it out. After a few laps I pulled back up to my mom and the others beaming ear to ear.

"Mom, I LOVE her!" I told her as I looked her right in the eye.

"So, you want to get her?" she asked with a smile, already knowing the answer.

My eyes got all big and I nodded my head up and down rather dramatically like a broken bobble head,

"YES!!!" I shrieked! Mom smiled; she just wanted me to say it.

She looked over at Corie and Tracy, hesitating but knowing what she was about to do,

"Okay…" she said slowly… lives changing with her words, "We will take her!"

I just collapsed on Pepper's neck and gave her a hug. Of course, Mom had brought cash and paid Corie on the spot for Pepper and signed the bill of sale. She also paid for Pepper's board for the following month. It was the middle of April so she was already paid up till the end of the month, but Mom wanted to have it all squared away anyway.

Everyone gave hugs and Tracy said I could use one of her spare saddles and a bridle until I could get my own. As we got in the car, my excitement was tempered with worry about the path ahead. But I couldn't let Mom know, I had to figure this out on my own.

As we got in the car Mom looked at me, wide eyed and full of disbelief.

"I can't believe we just did that!"

"I know Mom! Thank you, thank you, thank you!"

"You're welcome, Dolly. You have always wanted a horse and I am glad we could make it happen!" Dolly was her pet name for me, she was the only one who called me that. I reached over the seat and gave her a hug.

"Thanks, Mom" I whispered again.

We sat back up, stared at each other and my mom squealed again,

"Ah, we actually did that!"

"Oh boy…" she continued, "Now I have to tell your dad!"

We exchanged tense looks. I didn't want to be there for that conversation. But I knew it wouldn't matter, it was already done and Mom had figured out how to do it with her own money. Dad couldn't make me give the horse back. Pepper was safe with me.

Alex Tyson

Pepper's First Ride

Tracy invited me, along with April and Liz, to go on a trail ride the following day. The only trail rides I had been on were the rented ponies at a state park with a guide, this would be a *real* trail ride!

I tacked up in my borrowed tack that was admittedly a bit too large for me, and we set off down the dirt road they lived on.

I was in the back of the pack, and the ride started uneventfully. I don't remember much of what we talked out, most likely pleasantries and getting to know one another better.

The real action started when we were about a mile down the road and we pulled off onto a side street to make a U-turn, turning ourselves around to head back.
As soon as Pepper was facing towards home, she began this jitterbug dance and pranced around. I pulled back to calm her, and looked at Tracy as to what was the matter with my new horse.

"She is just excited to go back" Tracy said, a bit uninterested.

Pepper was definitely interested in going home and she started to dance around more and more. I had never felt this level of power from a horse before. The push from her hind end, how she was able to trot in place and dance around. The range of motion that she had, she was twisting her hips from side to side, tossing her head in the air so high her neck was about to hit my nose, all while thrusting herself into the air prancing faster and faster and faster. The school horses in lessons never did this.

"Easy, Pepper!" one of the other girls yelled in a not-so-reassuring voice.

"Sit back! Pull back!" someone else yelled.

I was sitting back, I was pulling back, but I was no longer riding a horse but a dragon! Before I knew it the prancing got more bouncy and quicker, I started to wonder, *is she cantering?*

"Whoa, Alex! Whoa!"

"Stop!" yells that I couldn't discern.

But I wouldn't whoa, I couldn't stop, my dragon horse was springing forth, and before I knew it, we *were* cantering, no, *galloping* towards home at breakneck speed!

Once I realized that Pepper was taking off and running for home, I looked behind me to see if the others were coming to rescue me. They were not. They were walking in my direction, not trotting, cantering, and certainly not *galloping* towards me to rescue me. I was on my own.

Why aren't they coming to get me? My heart sank, maybe they were not going to be good friends after all.

I had never, ever, galloped before; this was a new experience. We were going as fast as I had ever gone in my life!

Surprisingly, it did smooth out quite a bit, it wasn't so bumpy as when we started. There was power of course, and we were being propelled through the air by a force that was unlike anything else. Even so, as the stride got longer and faster, there was a stillness to it, it almost pulled you in, lulling you into some sort of false security.

Just go with it.

Give in.

As soon as I thought these things, I fought against it. What witchcraft was at play here? I can't go with it; I need to stop it!

But how?

I had read in a book somewhere three things about runaway horses, which, I was quite certain, I was now on.

I remembered this:
1. Emergency dismount was an option, you could vault yourself off and try to land on your feet.
2. Take and give the reins.
3. Runaway horses often head back to the barn.

I quickly weighed these facts in my head. Getting off probably wasn't a good idea, I had never practiced an emergency dismount before, so I most likely wouldn't be able to do it right. Also, we were going *so fast* I feared I would break my legs. The time to get off had long passed. Since I knew she was most likely running back towards 'home,' the barn, I just needed to stay on until then. In the meantime, I would try this take and give the rein business to see if I could slow her down.

I tried, I pulled back on the reins for a bit, then put them forward. It didn't seem to make a difference. I tried it again. Same result. Maybe I didn't know how to do it right, the book was rather simplistic in its instructions on how to do this, and we had never encountered anything close to this in riding lessons. I did persist, trying over and over again but to no avail. Pepper didn't, however, get any faster, so perhaps it was working a little bit. At least it wasn't making it worse. It wasn't long after I committed to staying on that I lost my first stirrup. I was pushing on my feet so hard in an attempt to sit back and pull back that I popped it right out.

Great, I thought, just what I need. I had luckily cantered without stirrups before this so I knew a little of what to do. But I also knew that I needed to get that stirrup back because I was at a way greater chance of falling without it. I picked my foot up to try and get it back, but, being an English stirrup, it was swinging everywhere erratically in time with Pepper's frantic stride. I tried again and this time felt my balance shift to the side, slipping off.

No way. You are NOT falling off like this! Not your first day on this horse!

I put both hands on her neck and pushed myself back into the middle of the horse.

Whew...you're ok!

And then the other stirrup popped out.

My heart sank as I realized that I was galloping down a road, on my new horse, that I couldn't stop, without stirrups. I was going to fall; I was going to embarrass myself in front of my new friends. I probably already did that.

But, as my stirrups banged along my legs and Pepper's sides, I actually felt a little bit better with no stirrups instead of one. I would have preferred to have both of them, but I felt more balanced now than when I was off kilter and shifted to one side. I knew my situation was still serious, I needed to keep my heels down, sit up straight, and stay in the middle of my saddle if I was going to survive this.

We speed along for what seemed like an eternity. At one point, I looked behind me again to see if anyone was coming, trying to catch up, but I was alone. Alone with the road, my running horse, and the thunderous sound of hoofbeats pounding on the packed dirt. I had only heard that sound in movies, now it was my turn to live it, albeit under duress.

I was almost starting to settle into my out-of-control, yet not actively dying state when I realized I wasn't alone on the road anymore. A red car was approaching me head on.
Ok, they don't want to hit you, just go straight.
I did and the car passed. A few moments later I heard a car coming behind me.

Don't look at it, stay straight!

Thankfully, the next car passed pretty wide on my left and got in front of me. I half expected Pepper to go faster after the car but she didn't.

These people probably think I am some crazy yahoo running down the road... they don't know I am in trouble!

We galloped on. A few more cars passed. I was not very familiar with the road so I didn't know how far we needed to go before we got to the barn. If she was going to the barn, that is. I hoped she was. The book said that she was. But the book also said to take and give the reins to slow down and that wasn't working very well either so, who knows?

Before too long I saw a pasture that bordered the road, it looked like the barn. Pepper started to drift towards it. It was the barn! Pepper leaned into a hard left turn as the driveway approached, which caught me off guard as she didn't slow down one bit to turn.

I started to feel myself slip off, the force of the turn sending me off the other side.

No,no,no,no, not when I am this close!

I did the trick I had done earlier and planted my hands on the neck and attempted to throw my body the other way. It didn't work!

I was slipping more off to the right, we weren't on a straight line like before, and Pepper was still turning left. I really thought I was going to slip off on the hard dirt road, but then, a ray of hope!

Pepper slowed down a little as she straightened out towards a lane that went to the barn. I tried again, summoning all of my strength to get myself centered on the horse again.

Ahhhhhhhhh!

Oooo!

Got it!

I was back upright again, but my joy was short lived. We were still running. Where were we going? Shouldn't we be slowing down now? Pepper started to do a hard lean again to turn. Where?

My head was still staring at her neck from our near fall, I snapped it upright to look where she was going now. What peril awaited me next?

The gate.

There was a small gate, barely wide enough for a horse and maybe four feet tall on hinges. It was attached to a bigger wooden fence that gated in the horse area from the outside. Once in the barnyard, there was a barn immediately to the right that went into a very large field.

Go through the gate Pepper, don't jump the fence!

For once she listened to my plea and slowed abruptly, almost to a stop, flinging my body onto her neck. She spun to the right through the gate., whacking my knee hard on the side post. I still felt all her energy, she wasn't going to stop. She might be headed to that big open field and then I will never stop her! I was already half off and we were as slow as we were going to be. Time to try that emergency dismount.

I used all of my energy to propel myself from the horse, held onto the rein and landed on my feet. I staggered for a second once I touched down, almost falling backward, before I over corrected and landed forward on my knees. I let go of Pepper's reins to catch myself with my hands so I didn't face plant in the dirt. Once I got reoriented, I looked for Pepper, who was surprisingly standing calmly by the hitching post, waiting to be untacked.

I went to stand up and a bolt of lightning shot through my chest and into my stomach. My heart hurt, I was struggling to breath. This wasn't butterflies of excitement, this was a heart attack! My shoulders started heaving from the effort to get air, and I looked around wildly for anyone to help me. Anyone!
But there was no one there.

Am I going to die alone?
Is this how I go out, a heart attack?

I felt hopeless, what could I do? Nothing. Nothing except try to breathe.

I sat in the dirt, hugging myself and rocking back and forth, struggling to breathe. I think I had seen in some movie people taking deep breaths, as deep as they could, so I tried that. Slowly, breath after breath, rock after rock I was able to calm down. My chest loosened up. I could breathe. I still felt sick, but I didn't feel like I was going to die anymore. I waited a little longer to make sure, before slowly getting up. *Still good… not dying*.

I looked up at the road to see if anyone had gotten back yet. Nope. Still alone. So, I untacked Pepper, and resolved to wait around for everyone.

Eventually they did come back, at a walk, and saw me standing by Pepper.

"There you are!"

"We were worried about you, but we didn't want to run after you and make Pepper run harder, we figured she would come back home." Tracy said.

I didn't know what to say,

"Yeah, she ran all the way here, I couldn't stop her, and she ran through that gate and then I got off. But after I got off, I couldn't breathe and felt like I was having a heart attack!"

Tracy gave me a puzzled look but then simply said,

"That's the adrenaline. Your body makes it to keep going when you are really stressed or in danger. After the danger passes it feels like that."

I had never heard of such a thing, but I certainly experienced it, so I just nodded my head.

I don't remember telling my mom about anything that happened that day. Maybe Tracy did, but Mom didn't know much about horses anyway, and I still showed up the next day to ride Pepper. Only this time, in the arena.

~Adult Reflections~

This story is a classic example of what *not* to do. When you get a new horse, it is always advisable to ride in the arena for a bit, get to know it, and then take it out, especially if you are not an expert rider.

Tracy was right that running after a horse could make the situation worse, but if I was in this exact situation now, I would have tried to stop the horse before it took off. I may have told the rider to get off or physically try to block the horse with mine to keep it from going home. I may have even dismounted myself to hold their horse while they got off. I might even trade horses and ride their horse back.

While I was trying to "take and give" or "half-halt," I definitely wasn't doing it correctly at the time. The time when it would have been most effective was *before* the horse took off. Also, before the horse took off, or got going into a full gallop, an emergency or "one-rein stop" would have been effective. Shortening one rein almost to the bit and then pulling it toward my hip, effectively forces the horse to move in a small circle, slowing its momentum. This would also be a good time to get off.

While this is good story now because only my ego got hurt that day, I was darned lucky. I got off at the right time-when she slowed down enough. If I'd attempted an emergency dismount at a gallop, I could have broken a leg—if not my head. I could have smacked into the fence. Worst case scenario—we could have been hit by a car—or I could have slipped off and then been hit by a car.

I was in way over my head with no idea what to do, and no help to figure it out. I still shudder a little when I think about all the things that could have gone wrong, and how utterly clueless I was.

You don't know what you don't know. Until you do.

Shenanigans on Pepper. Who knows what I was doing?

Alex Tyson

Now...Gallop!

On Purpose.

To say that my relationship with Pepper was off to a rocky start was an understatement. But I learned. Some of it wasn't actually learning, more like pure stubbornness and youthful ambition that doesn't always measure consequences. I can definitely say that I persisted, I rode Pepper every day.

My mom ordered me the Silver Fox English tack starter set from the State Line Tack catalog. It was the cheapest tack one could buy: a saddle, bridle, bit, and girth for about $175. The other items were almost useless, but the saddle was actually pretty good and correct. Having a saddle that fit gave me some confidence, and before too long my friends and I found ourselves going out on the road again. Maybe Pepper felt she'd made her point that *she* was in charge—or maybe she felt the change in my confidence. But she never tried to bolt home again so I didn't have the opportunity to practice bringing her back when she got excited like that.

About a month after buying Pepper, I tagged along on a big road ride that led to a local farmer's open field. He said that as long as we stayed in the lanes, out of the crops, we could ride on his property. I was excited to try this galloping thing again, this time on purpose.

If you're a rider, and you have the skills or the bravery (hopefully both) you should gallop in a group of people, in a huge open space, at least once in your life.

I grew up in Holly, Michigan; land of many woods that backed up to state land-and more woods. A place where the roads didn't follow any kind of grid system. One could start out north, go east, and then get end up facing west. I was used to nature, and I was used to solitude and a seemingly endless expanse of land, but not flat. Not in a straight line.

The field was thick with corn stalks, but there was a bare pathway for the farm equipment. That is where we started, and since it was late Spring, the corn was low enough that you could still see as far as you could in any direction. The path was too narrow for the five of us to gallop: me on Pepper; Tracy on a draft-cross called Braveheart; Corie on her new Thoroughbred mare Abbey; April on Bug, her paint pony; and Liz on Shadow, her Tennessee Walker. We walked, single file down the lane, not saying much. It felt a little like walking to the gallows.

What would happen this time?

Would I be able to stop?

These were logical questions but I didn't voice them, nor did I put much effort into solving them. I just rode on. We made a few winding turns through the corn, climbing a little with each switchback.

A hairpin turn revealed another level of the field, this part unplanted, vast and sloping gently upward to another hill off in the distance. It was like another world had opened up and sprawled out before our eyes. One by one the horses left the cornstalks behind and entered the edge of the field. Braveheart and Bug seemed to know what was coming, as they started prancing around and didn't want to stay still while Tracy explained the protocol.

"Stay behind me," Tracy said, pointing to the top of the ridge with one hand while holding her beast back with the other.

"Pull up at that ridge up there. Then we will turn around, run back, and pull up here and walk back the rest of the way."

I don't even think I nodded, but I certainly didn't complain or raise any opposition, nor did anyone else. Satisfied, Tracy gave a little nod, turned her horse around to face the ridge and let him fly.

And then I was flying.

Pepper bolted off after the others; it was the biggest acceleration I had felt in my whole life. It was all I could do to not be left sitting there on my butt and watching her run off without me. I threw myself forward, grabbed some mane, got into a two-point to stick with her, and held on for dear life. Once Braveheart took off, Corie and her horse were close on their heels, then somehow April and I found ourselves next to each other, with Liz bringing up the rear.

The sound. The power. The thunder of all those horses running together.

DA DA DUH-DAH DAH-DUH-DA-DA-DUH....

Dirt flew in every direction, the earth opening up and giving way to our horses in flight. The wind whipped my cheeks and tears streamed down my face from the sheer force of our speed against the air.

At first, I was as terrified as I had been when Pepper took off with me on our first ride. But I slowly started to realize a few things.

First, relative to the other horses, Pepper wasn't going that fast. Braveheart and Abbey were way ahead. April had started out with Bug next to me but had urged him on faster and was a good four lengths in front of me. Liz was definitely behind me but my position in the pack had slipped quite a bit, even though we were going as fast as I had ever imagined a horse could go, way faster than when Pepper took off before.

The second thing I realized is that while it would have been impossible to stop in this moment (I didn't know how and I wasn't going to try) I felt pretty good up here. The hoofbeats were echoing inside my chest, I could feel the reverberations all throughout my body, and I could hear Pepper's breathing take on a certain cadence. Unlike the last time, I kept both my stirrups. It was going to be okay.

The slope of the hill started to increase and I was getting closer and closer to the other horses. I sat back and tried to stop Pepper but wasn't getting the greatest results. Seeing this, Tracy, who had already slowed to a walk, placed her big tank of a horse Braveheart in my path. Pepper slowed down, easily yielding to his presence. At the time I didn't really realize what she did, and even if I did, I was too pumped up on adrenaline to say 'thank you.'

"Everyone good?" Tracy asked.

Everyone just nodded. Liz looked a bit more bewildered than me, even though she hadn't gone anywhere near as fast as everyone else. April had a look on her face like she was excited to go again and try for faster. Tracy and Corie had an expression that I had never seen before: happy at the wild events but yet unfazed.

There is more out there; I just don't know it yet, I thought again.

"Okay then, back to it, pull up at the corn."

Tracy whipped her war steed around and took off again. This time I actually asked Pepper to run, she complied easily, shooting forward to follow her barn mates back. I didn't ask her to go any faster, but I did sail back towards the corn trail with a little less fear.

We coasted along, feeling the pulse and heart of what a horse is made to do.

Rearing: A Saga

Rearing: the act of a horse putting all of their weight on the hind legs, while hoisting their front legs both off the ground and into the air, assuming a more human like, vertical body stance. This is the stuff of movies and TV glory: Roy Rogers and Trigger...*The Black Stallion*...*Spirit, Stallion of the Cimarron*. Every little girl who loves horses has been bombarded with images of majestic, rearing horses.
Pepper was blessed by Corie with this end-all, be-all of trick training.
She could, amazingly, rear on command!
How awesome was that?! Not only were all of my horse dreams coming true, but I had at my disposal the thing of dreams: the rear!
Corie had mentioned that Pepper reared on command when we bought her, but taught me how to do it two months later.
"To rear," she instructed, "You act like you are going to back up, pull back with the reins and squeeze with both legs..."
Her voice trailed off as she picked her eyes up to look at me in the saddle on Pepper to make sure I was paying attention. I was. My eyes were fixed on hers and I nodded in agreement. She continued,
"But you need to raise your hands higher up to the sky in a slightly jerky motion. You can repeat it if she doesn't do it. Once she rears just lean forward in a two-point like a jump, grab some mane, and hang on till she comes down."
I nodded and she motioned for me to try.

I sat back, pulled slightly on the reins but was careful to elevate their position to a more vertical, upward pull and squeezed with my legs. To my surprise…it worked!

Pepper's weight shifted backward and I felt her front legs reach toward the clouds. I leaned forward to and stay in good balance with her, if I didn't, I would have fallen backwards over her hindquarters. We hung in the air for a few moments, my lips pressed against her coarse mane, and I thanked the Lord above for all the magic in the world such as this.

It was over almost as quickly as it began, and we descended, literally, back down to earth.

"Good job!" Corie praised, "Just like that! You have it!" I had it.

"Now," Corie warned, her voice dropping down a bit, a serious tone breaking the magical spell,

"You have to be careful not to do this too much. For one, she could lose the cue, or on the opposite end, since it is so close to backing up, she might rear when you don't want her to. So only every once in a while." She looked at me with a look that said: *now I know you are not going to listen but I have to say it anyway because I am the adult.*

"I understand." But what is 'every once in a while?'

Once a week? Once a month? Few times a year? Who knows? I just knew it couldn't be every day. Fair enough, magic can't happen every day, then maybe it wouldn't be magic.

Alex Tyson

Preteen Boys

Our magic did find itself quite useful when on another road ride, Liz, April and I came across a rogue band of boys our age. Boys of eleven or so can be the cruelest creatures, testing boundaries and strength on unsuspecting victims. Worse if they are in a group. Doubly worse if they are on bikes.

And on bikes these terrorists were, as they sped around the corner, looking for trouble.

They came flying directly at us, peddling hard at full speed, leaning down into their bikes to keep their momentum, locking eyes on us girls with an evil glint in their eyes. We were in a terrifying game of chicken, only we wouldn't be able to move our horses fast enough, and it didn't look like they were slowing down. Almost instinctively, Liz and April moved their horses closer to Pepper and I, sandwiching me in between them, but in doing so creating a wall of horse flesh that the boys were bound to hit.

Not anticipating this, the boys slammed on their brakes and jerked their handlebars hard to the right, sending a spray of gravel and dirt into the horses. Our steeds didn't like this very much and jerked their heads up and shied away from the rocks to the left. We were spooked too, we didn't know what the boys would do, or how our horses would react.

The ringleader boy seemed to sense that his actions had caused some fear on our part and then began to change course and circle the bikes around us, getting awfully close to our horses' hind legs in the process.

Don't they know they could get kicked doing this? I should warn them...On second thought, maybe I shouldn't and one good kick will solve this problem.

"STOP!" I yelled as the leader boy crossed in front of me.

Surprisingly, he did stop, turning his bike away from his tight horse circle and looping back around to face us. He had this amused look on his face that I spoke up. How dare I defy him?

"Aww... you don't like us being here?" he taunted.

"Obviously, not" April snapped back.

"Well, you see, I do like being here. I hate these stupid horses, and you stupid girls that ride them!"

"Hey!" Liz squeaked out, she didn't know what to say or do really, but she was certainly offended.

The leader looked us up and down, he had a nasty smug grin and a mop of black hair that almost covered his eyes. I didn't really pay attention to the other boys because they just mimicked what the leader did. They were harmless sheep, unless their wolf called them to battle.

"You know since you don't like it so much, I think I will just throw some rocks at these stupid horses!" He spat at us, and started looking to the side of the road for a suitable weapon.

THAT WAS IT.

I had enough of this bully and his antics, and I was going to put a stop to it.

"Oh, yeah?" I asked him, "Well watch out, then!" Not the best comeback, but I was enraged. I stepped Pepper out of our horse shield toward the leader, and marched Pepper right next to his bike. He wasn't anticipating this and recoiled a little bit at my forwardness. I did the only logical thing that an eleven-year-old girl with a trick trained horse could do in this situation.

I asked her to rear. Right in his face.

Pepper, glorious Pepper, came through for me and reared as high as she ever had, towering over that bratty boy and put the fear he gave us, right back into him.

"Ahhhhh!" He screamed, not knowing what was happening, but clearly seeing that my horse was a lot bigger than him at the moment. He scrambled to get his bike out from under Pepper and her hooves which were easily over his dirty, moppy little head. I couldn't really see his face, but I like to think regret washed over it as he realized what he had done. A novel concept, actions and consequences. He had poked the bear. Or in this case, the girl.

Pepper landed from her rear a little sooner than I wanted her to, we needed to be a force to be reckoned with. I asked her to go up again, and she did. Pepper was not normally this compliant but I think she enjoyed the revenge. This really threw off the leader, who at this point now abdicated his position as king of the road and turned his bike around, screamed and told the others,

"She is crazy! Let's get out of there!"
They all turned and followed, peddling as fast as they could, looking over their shoulders as they did to make sure I didn't follow.

"AND DON'T EVER COME BACK!" I yelled after them, with a huge grin on my face.
When I turned back towards our group their mouths were hung open in disbelief. Did I really do that?

"Well, I don't think they will be back" Liz said, breaking the stunned silence.

"That was awesome!" April said with a smile. I did something right in the eyes of my new horse friends! For once in my life, I got to be the hero!

"Let's go just in case they change their minds and come back for more" I said, still a little worried about them, and my rage starting to wane.

We told every single soul that we could what happened, and how Pepper saved the day by rearing. The adults around us were impressed but a little worried. At least we weren't victims, and maybe those boys would straighten out a little by meeting a 1,000-pound animal up close and very personal.

~Adult Reflections~

No regrets on this one.

I gained a real sense of agency from taking charge in a difficult situation. I wasn't just going to take the threatened assault against me, I was going to fight back. I've been thankful ever since, that this ordeal showed me my strength. Sadly, I never got a picture of Pepper and I rearing. This was also a rare moment of unity with Pepper. As our adventures continued, she didn't rear when I needed her to, and did when I didn't. This will just be one glorious moment when my rage and Pepper's snarky nature came together at the right time, and sent me high, high into the stuff of magic.

This is fun?

That summer I went to a number of 4-H horse shows at our local county fairgrounds with April and Tracy. We didn't own a trailer, or a truck that could have pulled it even if we did, and they were nice enough to let us hitch a ride in their two-horse trailer. Our 4-H group also had a drill team, so we went every other week or so to practice. I quickly learned the lesson that horses are WAY different off the property then they are at home.

Pepper was a COMPLETY DIFFERENT HORSE and I had absolutely no clue how to handle it. She refused to stand in one spot, jigging up and down, swinging her hip this way and that into unsuspecting people. She held her head out and up, trying to get away from the control of the bit. She was faster, way faster, than she was at home. She freaked out whenever she couldn't see any of her stablemates.

She dragged me down the barn aisle a few times, stepped on my feet, and ran over me. Tracy suggested to us that we give her a calming supplement to try and chill her out, but it didn't seem to kick in until well after we were done showing. When it did, she practically fell asleep. I almost always got last place in my classes. When I finally beat one person in my class of six, getting a fifth -place ribbon, I was over the moon. I really didn't understand what to do, what the judges were looking for, or how to handle my anxious horse. Tracy was helping her daughter, and not being a trainer herself, didn't know how to help me. She just drove me there and offered help when she knew how. My mom wouldn't even hold Pepper-she was scared of horses in general-and particularly scared of Pepper when she was acting up. Frankly I really had no desire for my mom to help me with my horse, since she possessed absolutely no natural horse sense.

Once, while helping me give Pepper her pre-show bath, Mom decided that Pepper's face was dirty and needed to be cleaned. Her solution? Lifting the hose, and, at full power, spraying Pepper in the face.

Of course, Pepper was not having any of it and reared up to get away from the water spray.

"MOM STOP! STOP! MOM!" I yelled at her. She was hurting Pepper!

"QUIET!" Mom yelled back in frustration.

She then noticed a new target: Pepper's belly. While Pepper was in the air, rearing in desperation to get away from my mother, Mom aimed the hose at Pepper's exposed underbelly, washing that as well. When Pepper came back down my mom snapped at me,

"Make her do that again, it's really dirty down there!"

"MOM! NO!" I shrieked at her; I didn't have the words, I just got red faced and was about to explode.

Tracy came to my rescue, took the lead rope away from Mom and set it on the ground, guided her away from the horse, and explained the situation for me.

"Look Teresa… you can't do what you just did. That horse is very mad at you right now, you can't just spray an animal unexpectedly in the face, especially if it rears away from you in the process."

"But she rears with Alex!" Mom said, defensive.

"This is a little different…" Tracy's voice trailed away as she took my mom away from the scene of the crime.

I finished cleaning up Pepper, royally embarrassed at my mother's incompetence. How could she not know that? THERE ARE THINGS MORE IMPORTANT THAN CLEANING!

Upon her return Mom, as moms do, didn't apologize...but she also didn't do it again. I don't believe she actually ever understood why what she did was wrong. Pepper was a flea-bitten grey horse, and every little stain and piece of dirt showed. She was dirty. In Mom's mind, she was trying to do me a favor by cleaning her up. Needless to say, that was the last time Mom did anything to help with show prep. Other than do my hair and hand me things. No horse handling whatsoever.

This lack of help proved problematic at our local country fairgrounds, or "Hilltop" it was referred to. Hilltop has a huge show arena and a disproportionally small warm-up arena. Then, up a very steep hill, are the barns and the trailer parking. It is easily a five-minute walk, especially for a kid. Two minutes minimum if you ride up it.

Let's say I forgot something, my gloves for example, and realized right before I needed to go into the ring. My mom was not going to hold my horse while I ran back to the barn to get them. She is a slow walker, and wouldn't know where they were anyway. I would be late for the class (which you can't be) or have to go in without gloves. After some tense moments and screaming in frustration on my part, I learned pretty quickly that I had to take care of, account for, and remember EVERY SINGLE THING. Tracy was too busy to help, and my mom didn't know how. It was up to me. In some ways this had a great maturing and growing effect on me, as I learned a great deal of responsibility. On the other hand, it was quite anxiety inducing because I knew I couldn't rely on anyone, I had to figure everything out on my own. I didn't know what I was doing to begin with, so I was way more tense than I should have been, which didn't help out my already tense horse.

We were a disaster, really, and I wish I could look back and help younger me. I was so stressed out. But, as usual, I stubbornly continued, despite being miserable.

The county fair loomed at the end of the summer. April, Liz, and pretty much everyone else from 4-H was going to be there, and they promised that it would be fun.
Fun they said. Right.

Now I know that pretty much everyone but me that did 4-H ever LOVES the fair. It was the highlight of their year. And while they may have been over it when the week was finished, they maintained a love-hate relationship with it overall, coming back every year and remembering it fondly for the rest of their adult lives.

Not me.
I HATED IT.

Reasons that I hated fair:
1. My horse was a lunatic. If I thought she was tense going to the shows before, coop her up in a stall for a week and try it. Absolutely bonkers.
2. I could tell the adults around me were worried about my safety; people gave me weird looks. This really helps one's confidence.
3. EVERY SINGLE PERSON decorated their stall elaborately. I was not crafty, neither was my mom. We looked like the hillbillies of the group with our plain stall. I felt really left out.
4. It rained every day. My white horse was dirty. This furthered the hillbilly trope.
5. The highlight of the week was me jumping in the pouring down rain and slop soup that became the arena after a week of torrential downpour. Not because I did well…oh, no… because no one could believe that I rode through it, didn't scratch, and by some miracle stayed on. At the time I didn't get exactly what all the fuss was about. I thought they were impressed by my

bravery to jump in the rain, not scared by my lack of riding skills and apparent presence of a guardian angel.
6. Everyone camped at fair. We didn't have a camper and my mom refused to tent camp. Add to the feeling left out. So much happened socially after we left.
7. And finally, the two rearing…or lack of rearing incidents.

The only surviving fair pictures of Pepper and I.

The Time we Reared...and I Mean Reared

By day three of fair, it was pretty obvious that my horse was insane, hated being cooped up, and in no way shape or form could I expect her to behave for the class that I had the best chance in: Youth English Equitation on the flat. I knew this was the class that I might possibly place in. Judging was supposed to be on the rider, not the horse. While I didn't necessarily know all the nuances of showing, I had been told by a lot of people that I had good equitation skills, so I figured I would give it my best shot.

In order to have the best chance of success, I convinced my mom to drive me there early and drop me off, at five-thirty a.m. before the show started at eight. I would give Pepper the calming paste as soon as I got there, prayed it worked in time for the class, and in the meantime ride the absolute tar out of her beforehand. Slim chance, but I hoped she would be tired enough and behave. There would be no one in the warm-up pen that early, so I would have plenty of space and not freak anyone out with her antics.
It sounded like a perfectly good plan. Brilliant even.

But it wasn't... not even close.

My first mistake was not taking into account one of the reasons that Pepper was so amped and nervous: she wanted to be around her friends. Getting up early and taking her, alone, down the hill and completely out of sight of not only her friends but ANY horse cranked her anxiety level up to about eleven.

The ride started out in a series of rapid circles around the mounting block, with Pepper whipping to the side, whinnying, and running away from me any time I tried to put my foot in the stirrup. This went on for a good two minutes until I had finally had enough of it, jammed my foot in the stirrup, and lurched myself over her back while she took off as I remained forward to try and stay with her.

As soon as my torso collapsed on her neck she reared up in protest. While shocked at this escalation of events, I was already leaning forward, so I wasn't unbalanced. Once she touched back down, I kicked her forward into a trot, and regaining my other stirrup along the way.

Pepper WOULD NOT SHUT UP. She kept whinnying, hollering, at the top of her lungs, yanking her head in the air and hollowing out her back every time she did. She held her Arab tail up high and snorted loudly after every whinny, the sound of which was so booming it resembled a gun shot. Any attempts to canter were met with an odd sideways up and down gait that I couldn't quite place but it certainly wasn't a normal canter. Any attempt to walk was promptly met with sudden stops and rearing bouts.

Trotting was the only thing we seemed to be able to do. On and on we went, loudly, so loud that I was sure some adult would come out of somewhere and yell something about not being safe. They tended to do that when Pepper was rearing...

I am not sure how long I trotted around, but it was long enough to have enough sweat on her that warranted a bath before the show. Great, more work. While I'd certainly made no progress in tiring her out, *I* was exhausted. I couldn't trot anymore. I knew it would be a bad idea to trot up the hill to the barn, risking another bolting scenario, so I needed Pepper to walk so we could go back to the stall.

But Pepper was not about to walk, nor stand for me to get off. I wasn't sure what to do, I had never gotten off a moving horse before and stayed upright. Much less a horse that is bound to move in any and all directions, including sideways.

"Walk, Pepper," I told her in my tired, agitated voice.
We reared.
"WALK!" I yelled.
Another rear, this time a little higher.
"I SAID WALK!" I screamed at the top of my lungs, angrily hammering my hands toward my knees on the reins down in frustration.

In retaliation, Pepper gave me the biggest rear I had ever rode.

We lifted high into the air, her hooves now the height of a person standing upright. I flung myself up on her neck to stay with her, holding mane for dear life. We hung there, suspended upright for what seemed like forever. I even felt Pepper teeter backward a little bit, she was that straight up. She was no longer a twenty-five-year-old sway-back mare but a young filly in her prime showing off all her strength and athleticism. I was astounded by what I was riding, and wanted to see if there was anyone witnessing this spectacle, but I was too scared to leave my death grip on Pepper's neck to look around.

When we finally came back down to earth, I suddenly felt my leg give way under me, straightening rapidly as my stirrups seemed to become a lot longer.

Had I broken the stirrup leathers when she reared?

Ironically, when Pepper finally put all four feet on the ground she stood as still as a statue. Once I realized she wasn't going to go up anymore, her muscles calm and relaxed, I went about investigating the stirrup situation. I noticed that my feet were still in the stirrups, and the leathers didn't appear to be broken.

I lifted my leg up from the flap and saw something that I had never even heard of, and still haven't since.
She had reared so high, and been up there for so long that the stirrup leathers came out and off the bar.

English saddles have a metal bar that is attached to the tree, or hard frame of the saddle. This bar runs horizontally, and a stirrup leather is shimmied between the saddle leather and the bar; and that is what the stirrup is anchored to. The bar has a moveable piece at the back, which is usually kept straight or can be pushed upwards. When left straight, in the default position, it is designed to release if a rider is dragged behind a horse with his or her foot caught in the stirrup helping to avoid injury. This is where it is 99% of the time. When jumper riders get close to jumping four-foot fences, they put the bar up so that the arc of the jump at that height doesn't push the leathers off the bar in mid-air. They risk their foot getting caught, but it's either that or no stirrup. Since I wasn't jumping that high, mine were kept straight.

What happened astonished me. My leathers were off the bar, but still on my feet because the leather had folded over between where the keepers and my legs were, awkwardly but precariously holding it in place. Whether it was the individual saddle design, my conformation, how I was pushing on the stirrups, the rear alone, or combination thereof I will never know.

All I did know was that I had ridden close to 100 rears that summer in that saddle, mostly accidental, and this had NEVER happened.

I instantly knew what this meant. I was near vertical. Pepper could have flipped over.

I was spooked, I got off and took the leathers in hand with me as I walked up the hill. I needed to clean them before my class anyway.

Flipped. I could have flipped over and broke my neck. Died even. What was I getting into?

I could feel the adrenaline flooding my system again as I made my way up the hill, Pepper in tow but fixated on the approaching horses. I was even shaking a bit as I held the reins. How could she go that high? I was scared of the rear, or rather what could happen if she reared that way again, but I was more scared of Pepper herself. If she is capable of that, what else would she do? I knew that it was a rite of passage in some ways to experience these crazy things, but maybe I had gone too far. I had crossed the line.

This was getting a little dangerous.

And yet, I couldn't help but be a little emboldened, despite the fear.

I felt a surge of confidence for the next big class at fair: the costume class.

~Adult Reflections~

One word: groundwork. I needed to know what it was and how to do it. This would allow me to handle Pepper better, expose her to new situations safely, and establish myself as the leader. Clearly, Pepper derived no comfort from my presence, and was looking out for herself. At a minimum, I needed to know how to move her shoulder and hips away from me, cue her to move her head down, and how to lunge. groundwork could have helped me turn the tide on this one, but at the time I didn't even know what ground work was.

I clearly didn't understand horse behavior and thought I was going to muscle my way through a situation that I should have thought my way out of. Pepper wasn't "being bad," she was scared and wasn't getting any direction from me. Horses are herd animals; being alone is scary business to a horse unless they see you as the leader of the herd. I was no leader, but a clueless passenger who thought running her around would solve my problems. While blowing off some energy on the lunge line might have helped, and certainly would have been a safer option, the root of the problem was Pepper's anxiety about being in strange surroundings and away from her buddies. It takes lots of hard work and desensitizing to change this behavior and get the horse more comfortable. Running around alone in a ring is not the solution.

Most rears are only a few feet off the ground, waist high on a typical adult at most. Vertical rearing is nothing to joke about. I still have never heard of anyone else's stirrups coming off of bars, but I have seen horses flip over backwards or tip over sideways as a result of vertical rears. Many times. And too often an ambulance came to rush the rider to the hospital. In one case, the rider snapped her femur and had to have a metal rod put into her leg. In each of those instances, the riders were pulling back on the reins instead of leaning forward for balance at the height of the rear, and essentially flipped their horse over.

Circus folk and their performing horses can rear this way often, but if you really pay attention, you'll notice they are not high and straight up and down from nose to tail, often there is a "V" shape between the ground and the horse's body angle, offering more stability. If you ever find yourself in this situation lean forward, grab the mane, even bear hug the neck if you have to, but under no circumstances should you pull the reins towards you.

The Time We Really Needed to Rear... and Didn't

As I said before, I am not an artsy person, although I have always admired them. My mind turns to more practical things, rather than how to decorate. But, when you're a kid, and you have this older person mentality, it does set you apart from the other kids. In order to somewhat combat this, I was going to do the costume class at fair. I had determined that I would be an angel and Pepper would be the devil (no animosity there). My mom had suggested, somewhat rightly, that Pepper, being almost white, should be the angel and I should be the devil. But...Pepper was some form of the devil in my eyes, so the shoe fit. My costume was not that elaborate, Mom got a cheap white dress with a flimsy wire halo that went on my head for me, and Pepper got a black blanket with some red glittery devil horns that I put under her bridle.

I knew that my costume was not all the rage, nor would it ever have a chance to be. Even if I had my mom do it completely, it still would not be up to snuff with what the other mothers could come up with. No, my crowning glory would be my routine that I would perform.

I had music to go with my performance, and I based my routine on some of the drill team exercises that we had done over the summer. I had choreographed circles of various sizes and speeds, diagonal lines and lots of transitions. But the kicker, the big finale, the thing that people would remember happened at fair for years to come was I was going to rear at the very end! When the music reached its crescendo Pepper would rise into the air as the majestic devil that she was and wow the judges!

To add an extra bit of pizzaz I planned to smile and wave while we were airborne! It would be spectacular and everyone would remember it for all time! No one would do it except me. I didn't know anyone else who had a rear-trained horse. Pepper also certainly has the practice of rearing that week following the mega-rear the other day. I felt confident in being able to ride whatever she gave me.

April was doing the costume class as well. All of the participants were in the ring together, in the middle, and people had to do their routine at one end of the ring by the exit gates, and then leave once their routine was done.

My turn came before I knew it. Now was my chance to do something, anything, better than everyone else. This was my moment. No one else had a rearing horse, and Pepper reared at the slightest urging. I had even practiced the wave like Roy Rodgers on occasion. I had this.

I did my routine the best I could, I knew not all the circles were exactly circular, some were much more like ovals, but they were round. My speed changes were not as crisp as I wanted them to be. Pepper broke down to trot when I wanted her to go into a slow canter, and I am pretty sure I got the wrong canter lead going to the right.
But no matter!

The music was building, I made a loop to arch over and face the judges. I looked them right in the eye, they weren't going to believe it! I pulled up Pepper to a halt, took a brief moment of composure and asked her to rear...
Nothing

Absolutely nothing, she didn't even lean back and bob her head like she was thinking about rearing.
She felt like a normal horse, not like my crazy, athletic, bursting beast that I knew. In that moment, she was a twenty-

five-year-old nag of a horse with one foot in the grave. She felt like she was going to fall asleep.

I started to panic, I was running out of time, the music was almost over! I must have looked like a complete idiot asking a horse to rear who looks like she has absolutely no clue what you are talking about. To the naïve onlooker, it must have looked like I was trying to get her to back up.

Look at this girl, can't even back her horse up!

I could almost hear them in my head.

I tried again. Come on Pepper, I know you can do it! You are a crazy horse and rear ALL THE TIME. You know this! You got this!

Crickets.

The music ended, I could have cried, my one chance to shine at something.

Gone. Zip. Nada. Done.

I heard dismal clapping from my mom and Tracy as I left the ring. I hadn't told them my plan (I never really told any adults any of my plans so they couldn't stop me) but they probably thought that I just did bad. I had to tell them. Pepper just wouldn't do it.

As I went out of the ring, I marched right up to them to let them know that I had tried to do something life changingly awesome and cool, but it had failed,

"She wouldn't rear" I snapped a little too curtly.

"Oh?" Tracy asked.

"Yeah, I was gonna rear at the end like we have done hundreds of times! But she wouldn't do it!"

"Well, sometimes they just don't want to" Tracy replied. Which was true, obviously, but not what I wanted to hear.

"But she *always* does it!" I whined, about to cry. Couldn't they see I just wanted to be good at something. Just this once?

"Well, stop whining about it, Alex!" Mom scolded, "She just didn't want to do it this time!"

I huffed as I turned and walked away to find a spot to watch April's routine. They didn't understand.

I don't remember much about April's routine, but I do remember what happened at the end. As the music came to a point, April sat back, raised her hands and her horse reared! She reared high as the clouds and April had the biggest smile on her face and she turned to the side slightly, looked at the judges, and waved.

NO ACTUAL WAY.

Gasps from the crowd, then thunderous applause and hoots and hollers when they realized it was on purpose. People loved it. They loved it! April was beaming ear to ear, and living my dream! She must have thought the fact that Pepper reared was cool and sought to do it herself. Corie was at the barn all the time so she could have helped her in secret, as she was the one who taught Pepper, and we definitely didn't always ride together.

I knew April rearing had nothing to do with my lack of rearing, but I was SO MAD. I knew that it was wrong for me to be mad at her in this situation; so, I left quickly before she came out, put Pepper back in her stall, and changed out of my stupid costume.

That was it. Owning a horse was simultaneously the best thing that had ever happened to me, and nothing like I thought it would be. I was so discouraged, and none of the adults seemed to see how frustrated I was. Maybe, I thought, this just isn't for me.

To add insult to injury, the next day I was walking Pepper up and down the barn aisles to get some exercise when she bolted, dragging me behind her. Dogs barked at us and mothers pulled their toddlers close as we stormed down the aisle. After about fifty feet of bolting and dragging, she turned hard into the stall at a run and I realized I was going to get pinned between her hip and the door frame. I let go of the rope so as not to get smashed and in doing so faceplanted in the nasty sludge of the barn aisleway.

    Fair was terrible.

Swimming

Life went on after Fair. I resolved to NEVER do it again, and horse showing in general was even on the chopping block at this point. As a child, I couldn't explain to the adults around me, but I was scared, I didn't know what to do or what to focus on, and I wanted to do well. It wasn't about winning; it was about the approval that I was a good rider doing the right thing. I just never got it. I needed so much structure and so much more supervision. At the time, I would have for sure suggested the opposite.

One good thing that happened that summer is I got better at galloping. I had learned to get up off Pepper's back, which simultaneously made it easier for her to run and easier for me to stay balanced while she was running. I eventually got to the point where I could urge her into what I knew was her top speed. At top speed Pepper still wasn't the fastest, but I could now keep pace with April and Bug pretty well, occasionally beating them. I no longer had problems stopping or controlling Pepper when we ran, and it felt good to feel at ease with something that was once terrifying.

We were like feral children, running our horses at least once a week. We got good, but our horses got tired.
That summer I checked off another horse-related bucket list item: swimming.

Yes, swimming.

There was a pond in the horse's pasture at the farm. Some of the horses liked to go in and swim of their own accord. We took to swimming after we'd galloped the horses. Run for a mile or so, walk back, and then take them swimming. They must have been exhausted, but we did it all the time, no one stopped us, much less the adults. Our horses could have drowned for sure. To swim safely, you need to consider the ground conditions and potential sinking factor wherever you are swimming, which of course we had no concept of. Luckily, this somewhat newly manmade pond had a strong base and the horses never sank.

If you have never swam on a horse, it is a unique feeling. Whenever I remember the swimming we did, I always go back to the first time.

We were bareback of course, shoeless, and had changed into shorts. Pepper confidently went down the gentle slope of the water until it was about chest high, and my feet started to get wet. She kept descending, the water getting higher and higher, over my knee, then to my waist.

Still deeper she went, the water starting to close in around my arms and Pepper started to raise her head, picking it up and forward to stay out of the water. I leaned forward, and shoved my hands towards her ears so she could keep her head above water.

"Are we swimming yet?" I yelled out to the others, a little scared as I didn't want Pepper's head to go under, and we were so close to that, the water skimming her jawbone by this point.

"Oh, you'll know!" someone called back.

What on earth does that mean? I hate when people say that...

And just like that, I knew we were swimming. It feels like the whole world drops out from under you, like you are truly floating on a cloud. The "cloud" is the gap of water that is filling between your legs and the horse's side floating you ABOVE the horse! You are on the horse and above it at the same time! But, since the horse is moving forward, the water is pushing you backward off the back of the horse!

I realized this very quickly and gripped on the mane for dear life as my legs were no longer under me but going behind me, over Pepper's rump, I was floating parallel to and above the horse!

This magic didn't last very long though, as soon as Pepper's feet touched the ground again, while still pretty submerged it is easy to get back into the normal riding position, and you float no more.

We exited the pond dripping wet from head to toe, save a little bit on Pepper's face.

I am pretty sure I just started laughing.

Pure Joy.

This was living.

Then I did it again and again, chasing that feeling until some adult told me to stop.

It was the most wonderous thing, and I have swum horses many times since and still experience the same elated, euphoric feeling.

Pepper never told me no, at least not with swimming. Maybe she felt in sync with me then, or maybe she was just too tired to protest.

~Adult Reflections~

While it's not bad to swim a horse, and it is the most glorious, unearthly feeling, it is easier than you might like for a horse to drown. A horse can walk around in the water pretty much indefinitely; true swimming- water level over the horse's head- you have to monitor your horse's fitness level to be able to ascertain what is too much for them. If you're wrong in the middle of the lake, well, the results are disastrous.

Pepper and I swimming.

The Oxer

While I had no supervision, lessons, or help with Pepper, I was still taking lessons once a week on Haverhill's school horses.

Thank the Lord I was still able to do that. I had lots of new experiences on Pepper, but most of those experiences came with no direction on how to improve them.

It is so very different when you have your own horse versus riding other people's horses. Especially horses that are in a constant work program like lesson horses.

While I didn't improve much with Pepper, I was improving quite a bit in my jumping lessons. I had switched trainers, was jumping higher, and starting to jump more complicated courses. I rode a different horse nearly every time, and I was quickly becoming one of the better riders in my group.

Riding lessons were different, they were structured, and there was always someone to explain what to do and what not to.

I started to jump verticals (jumps with a rail straight across) instead of the smaller, more inviting cross-rails, and began to learn about the different types of jumps. One of these was the oxer. An oxer is a spread jump where there are at least two rails. In a typical ramped oxer, there are two sets of jump standards, or the posts that hold the poles. The sets are parallel to each other, a little spread out so the horse has to jump the width of both of the poles. The back pole is higher than the front pole, so the horses is jumping both height and width at the same time. As my instructor was explaining this to us, she was careful to point out,

"You always have to jump it in the direction of the smallest rail going up. You NEVER jump it from the top rail going down. The horse will not see the bottom rail and won't arch properly, leading to the horse not jumping the width correctly and crashing into the bottom rail."

She looked at us for understanding. We just stared at the oxer, afraid to jump it let alone jump it backwards.

"NEVER DO THAT. Got it?" she asked.

"Ok," we all said back in unison. We understood.

Jumping had a lot of rules, and strict adherence to them was paramount. You always called your jump lines with other riders, you always rode your corners, you always got out of people's way when jumping, you didn't go too fast, you always released over the jump, your two-point needed to be perfect, and you NEVER jumped oxers backwards.
Until I saw Corie do it at our barn.

I respected Corie. She seemed to know how to do nearly everything: she jumped well, galloped well, trained horses to rear and do tricks, and just had a general ease around the horses. Tracy seemed to turn to her for help when she needed it, and the other girls at the barn always seemed to ask her questions. I knew all these things, so when I saw her lunge her horse, Abbey, over an oxer backwards, I was shocked.

Corie seemed not to care at all about the rules of jumping. Every one of my instructors at Haverhill would have screamed their head off at her. Everyone knew not to do that! She was also lunging, sending the horse in a medium circle around her, so the horse approached the oxer at a pretty extreme angle before she had to jump it on a curve. In my past experiences, people had always approached jumps head on, pretty straight, and this seemed to be the norm. I kept waiting for Abbey to stop because of the sharp angle, or to hit the back rail, or to look concerned about the whole ordeal.

But Abbey didn't seem concerned at all. In fact, she seemed very confident, balanced, tucking her knees up high and being careful yet bold over the jump in typical Thoroughbred fashion. She was truly and utterly magnificent, rulebreaker and all.

Tracy was also watching this happen and didn't say anything to Corie either about their rule breaking. Maybe neither of them had heard of the rule? I didn't say anything, fearing that I was in fact the ignorant one. As I sat there and watched Abbey jump that oxer backwards, over and over in the circle, then turn around and jump in the correct way again and again, I was beginning to think that the people at Haverhill were wrong and that Corie was right. There wasn't anything to worry about, the horse was fine. She was happy to be jumping, and it didn't seem to matter either way whether her oxer was correct or backwards. Maybe there wasn't even a correct way to do an oxer? Everything was fine and people had made an awful fuss about nothing!

Realizing this, I did what any kid that knows it all would do–I was going to do the same thing. It can be done, so I will do it.

I still felt a little guilty about trying the "wrong thing" so I waited a few days until no one was around to make my attempt.

I eyed the oxer, which was bigger than most jumps I had done before, but I had just seen Abbey do it, so it was going to be fine. I warmed Pepper up, walk, trot, and canter both directions and she felt pretty good and calm. There was another smaller jump on the opposite side of the ring that I went over a few times as a warm-up. Once I was satisfied that we were good to go I eyed the big oxer. Or in this case the big backwards oxer, as it never occurred to me to try and jump it right ways first. No, this was an experiment and we had to get right down to it.

I still followed the rule of making a courtesy circle before the first jump. I knew I needed to have a pretty good pace going if I was going to make it, so I used the circle to urge Pepper up into a pretty brisk canter.

We kept our momentum as we headed straight a good six strides away from the oxer. Pepper's ears had locked onto to the jump, when that happens you can feel this commitment under the saddle in their back, a resolved stiffening that means the horse is preparing to jump.

A little bit of leg for encouragement on stride five, to keep the energy. The last three strides felt good, powerful and forward.

Three, two, one, liftoff!

Pepper rose as high as I had ever jumped in the air. We soared. It felt good to have some easy communication with Pepper and do something hard as a team. I felt balanced, centered, and confident.

People really needed to learn to let go of all of their rules and just live a little, have some fun. Rules are just to keep people in order, it doesn't really matter.
Jumping lasts a second and yet an eternity. The powerful thrust of takeoff, the hangtime of being airborne, all four feet off the ground rounding over the obstacle, feels like forever, in this space absent from time. The descent feels much the same, you know you are going down but it doesn't feel super quick. Only when their hooves touch back down to earth does time speed up again.

But this time, something was different. As we started to go down from the jump, I noticed that something was off.

The arch of the jump is supposed to be even, and it feels that way too. The takeoff spot and the landing are usually of equal distance, and equal angle. But this was different, there was a twist in Pepper's side that I never felt before, and instead of arching down she was going straight down, to the ground, almost as if she was diving towards it. I realized we *were* diving for it; we were going to the ground! Pepper was falling and I was going with her. Pepper had twisted so far that her body was near parallel to the ground as her neck hit first.

THUD.

Upon impact I was shot off in front of Pepper, luckily to the side. I was able to get up quickly and saw the horror of what followed.

After her neck hit, Pepper rotated upward slightly onto her right shoulder and then skidded on her side through the dirt and grass another few feet closer to me. While skidding her back feet remained in the air over her head for what seemed like forever. When she finally stopped sliding, her hind legs smacked the ground with another loud thud. She laid there flat on the ground. Not moving.

"PEEEEEPPPPPPPEEEEEEERRRRRR!" I screamed and immediately got up and ran over to her head.

She didn't respond to my yell, lying motionless in the dirt. I killed my horse!

But she was still alive, I found when I got to her head. She was breathing, her eyes were open, blinking. She was alive but immobile, still, and unmoving.

What about her legs? Were any of them broken?

I left her head to look at and feel her legs. Nothing looked broken, there were no bones sticking out and none of her legs seemed swollen. She didn't have any cuts. While inspecting her back legs I looked back at the jump, poles scattered everywhere. A big flat drag mark on the dirt and grass where she fell down and slid to where she lay now.
I am such an idiot. How could I have done this? How could I be so stupid and hurt Pepper?

No one was even home at the time. I wanted to call the vet because I knew that even though she was breathing, she might be dying. I couldn't call anyone as I didn't have a phone. The house would be locked and there wasn't a phone in the barn. I just had to wait until someone came back. Pepper had trusted me and went over the jump, we felt so good going over it, and then I sent her to her doom! I am a terrible person, a terrible rider, and I killed a horse. Who kills a horse? I wallowed and cried and cried, about the death of my horse and the death of all future possibilities. I loved horses. I loved riding. I loved this life I was living. But I ruined it. I ruined it!

I walked back over to Pepper's head, and sat down in the grass. I lifted her head and put it into my lap. She didn't protest. I just stroked her big head, which seemed so much bigger now that we were on the ground and I was cradling it. I just stroked and stroked her, shaking, trying to ground myself with the movement, pressing firmly into her face as if it would revive her. Uncontrollable sobs filling the hopeless silence.

I cried until snot filled up my whole face and I could barely breath. Presented with a lack of air I started to hyperventilate. Gasping for air and feeling so overwhelmed at all of the emotions I had never felt before, a guilt that weighed down on my lungs and wouldn't allow me to breathe.
The gasping must have stirred Pepper, and she picked her head up, rolling onto her shoulder and sat with her head upright.

I stopped crying out of shock and backed away from her and stood up myself, hoping she would follow me. She swung her head back and forth a bit, gaining momentum, and then stuck her left front leg in front of her, then her right. She launched her head forward and down to pick her body up, and after a few wobbles on her back feet she was standing! I wrapped my arms tightly around her neck in joy!

You're up!" I shrieked. But then I wondered could she walk? Was she still hurt?

I gently took the reins over her head, holding them loosely and walked in front of her, willing her forward, watching her legs like a hawk for a limp. By some miracle there wasn't one; Pepper seemed fine. In fact, she seemed as if she had just awoken from a nap. I made my way to the barn, took off all of Pepper's tack, and walked her around until my mom came to pick me up about an hour later. In that time, we stopped, backed up, did circles both directions, and even trotted both ways. She never limped and didn't hesitate. I knew that she was all right in spite of me.

Pepper's skid mark stayed in the arena for a while until it finally rained. No one seemed to notice or asked me about it. I even left the poles scattered there, telling on myself and almost hoping someone would punish me. I had done a bad, bad thing, the worst kind of thing. Even though there wasn't any permanent damage I had hurt my horse, and I had hurt her unnecessarily. I was reminded of the squire in *Black Beauty* who broke his horse Ginger's leg foxhunting recklessly. I felt like that squire, I was reckless. I shuddered every time I passed that skid mark until the rain washed it away from view. I gave Pepper lots of extra carrots and didn't even want to jump or gallop her anymore. I couldn't be trusted to make the right choice so I just was going to ride around, plainly, where I couldn't hurt her. I knew deep down I wouldn't be this way forever, but there needed to be a way for me to make decisions and not be reckless. I didn't trust my own judgment. And the rules of jumping still didn't make sense.

~Adult Reflections~

This was almost a life changing event in the worst possible sense.

First, I should have never been in this situation to begin with. One of the first rules of riding is: no jumping without a trainer present in a lesson. Period. There is so much that can go wrong and so much that one doesn't know.

Second, obviously, I shouldn't have jumped the oxer backwards, and the adults present shouldn't have done it, even if it worked out ok for that individual horse. I shudder to think how close I came to killing Pepper (or myself for that matter) or permanently injuring one or both of us. I would be a completely different person if my carelessness had led to the death or maiming of an animal. I never want a kid to be in the same position I was in, ever; not on my watch.

On a positive note, I learned. I was truly remorseful, and I had a newfound reverence for what trainers, books, and more experienced people had to say. The rules were there for a reason, even if I didn't understand them. Moving forward, I at least always *considered* the rules. I sometimes thought the rule didn't apply to me, which led to its own problems.

But I never again completely tossed out the rules.

Inconsiderate Cleaning

My mom is a fanatical cleaner. Our house was always ready for company; there was no such thing as clutter, dust, dirt, or grime. Mail was not left on the table; shoes were never strewn about. The place always looked like a bed and breakfast. How my mom did this I will never know. She worked a full-time job and carted me around, but the house was spotless, even with two dogs that shed. I would truthfully be totally comfortable eating off the floor. Whenever I asked her why she did it, or how, I would always get a very simple response:

"I just like to clean."

At Tracy's barn, the rule was that you had to clean your own stall at least every other day. Her stalls did not have mats, and she insisted that boarders use pelleted shavings instead of the big flake shavings. Her reasoning was she had limited compost space and the flake shavings took up too much room. Pellet shavings broke down into finer pieces, and in her opinion, composted better.

The thing about stalls that do not have mats is that they have to be bedded deeply to ensure the horse won't get sores from laying on the uneven, hard, stall surface, packed down tight from horses being in it day after day. Just the horses walking around and moving will tear up the dirt and cause high and low spots. The other thing about matless stalls is they are harder to clean. The surface you are scooping from is not flat, and sometimes, in an attempt to get all the pee out, you end up taking some dirt with you from the base, further adding to the unevenness problem.

Since I did it every day, I had figured out how to get around these issues, how to spread the bedding out evenly, what was pee and what wasn't, and even how to make the dirt a little more level when I could.

The problem came in the fall when I went back to school and got sick. I was totally out for the count. It took a lot for me not to want to go to the barn, but I was sick for a week, home from school, and just sitting on the coach with chicken noodle soup. A trip to the doctor revealed I had bronchitis, something I got just about every year from my dad smoking in the house.

Mom told Tracy I was sick, and that she would take up the task of cleaning Pepper's stall until I got better. No problem.

But Mom did not understand the nuances of horse keeping, that fill dirt was hard to come by, and that having uneven floors in stalls is a bad thing for a lot of reasons and hard to fix. No, she just saw pee that seeped into the dirt. It was dirty. It needed to come out.

The first day she took out buckets and buckets of dirt that was also mixed with urine, creating a crater near the back of the stall. Tracy called her later that day,

"Hello?" Mom asked all chipper.

"Hey Teresa, It's Tracy from the barn."

"Oh, hi Tracy! What's going on?"

"Hey I called to tell you that when you are cleaning the stall for Alex, don't dig up the dirt."

"The dirt?" Mom was so confused.

"Yeah, the dirt. At the back of the stall there is a big hole with a bunch of dirt missing."

"Oh, okay," Mom continued, confused, "I thought I was just taking out all the pee."

"Well, you got all the pee, but you also took out a bunch of dirt at the back and now the stall is uneven."

"Oh... sorry," Mom paused, "I guess I'll do better next time."

"Thank you, Teresa, talk to you later."

When Mom hung up, I could tell that she didn't really understand what was going on, but I didn't think too much of it.

The next day Mom went back and she did it again, this time Tracy was there while she was cleaning, probably skeptical that my mom would do it right this time.

"So, this is dirt," Tracy walked into the stall and pointed at the shovel full of wet dirt that my mom had in her hands.

"But it looks like pee?" Mom asked, perplexed.

"Well, there might be some pee in there, but it is mostly dirt."

Mom looked but didn't understand. In her mind, pee is pee.

"And see how uneven this is now?" Tracy pointed to the low back of the stall that was at least a foot deeper than the rest of the stall,

"I have to bring in new dirt and level this now, your horse can't stand in something this uneven all night," she huffed, frustrated.

"Okay," Mom answered, though in her mind, uneven footing was a small price to pay for cleanliness. I truly thought she believed that Tracy should do this, and that it was part of the boarding fee, since the stall had pee-soaked dirt.

Later in the week when I felt well enough to go to the barn, Mom and I would do chores together, so I could help but also get my strength back. At the barn there was a rather large white board that people used to make announcements, leave phone numbers, papers, and the like. Upon walking into the barn my mom got so red faced I thought she was going to turn into a tomato. The source of her horror was the white board, filled to every corner with large capital letters that stated:

TERESA! YOU HAVE TO STOP TAKING ALL OF THE DIRT OUT OF THE STALL. YOU ARE NOT LISTENING. THERE IS A HUGE HOLE IN THE BACK THAT IS GOING TO COST ME OVER $100 TO FIX. YOU ARE NOT RESPECTING MY PROPERTY OR YOUR HORSE. STOP NOW OR BE FORCED TO LEAVE!

Well, that was crystal clear. I didn't know what was happening so I walked over to the stall and sure enough, there was a hole in the back of the stall that was about knee deep.

"Mom, why did you do this?" I asked, concerned

My mother is a patient lady, but she snapped at me,

"I DON'T KNOW, ALEX! THERE IS PEE EVERYWHERE, THE HORSE CAN'T STAND IN PEE. SHE WANTS OUR HORSE TO STAND ON DIRT THAT IS SOAKED IN PEE AND I WON'T HAVE IT. THE DIRT SHOULD COME OUT, AND IT SHOULD BE REPLACED BECAUSE IT. IS. DIRTY!"

I had never seen this type of outburst from my mother so I didn't say anything, I just started cleaning the stall myself. I tried in vain to even out the stall but the hole but it was simply too large. It was essentially now the whole back half of a 12X12 stall. I cleaned the stall quickly, and Mom just went and sat in the car.

What was happening?

I was inclined to think that my mom was in the wrong, but I also had never seen her so angry and that counted for something. I had a sense that we should get out of there, quickly, before Tracy saw my mom. I finished everything up, got the stall set up for night feeding, and left.

The entire way home Mom talked about the injustice that had been dealt to her,

"How dare she put that on the white board for all to see? How embarrassing!"

"She won't put mats in those stalls! They need mats so they can be cleaned properly! "

"I would have even bought the mats!"

"You know Alex, when we get home, we are going to look for another barn, this just isn't working out anymore!"

She meant it. Dead serious. When we got home, she continued her fervor through the front door, up the stairs, and all the way up to my room.

"Where is that local horse magazine that you have?" she looked around, desperate, eyes darting around my room for it. I went to the side of my bed where there was a stack of horse magazines and began thumbing around for it. Finally, I found it, *Saddleup! Magazine*, a Michigan and Ohio publication that listed trainers, barns, and events that was given out to feed stores every month.

"Find someplace else around here! Now!" she snapped. I did what she said and opened up the magazine. A few pages in was a full-page ad for a place called Wind Row. It was in Holly, where we lived!

"Look this one is in Holly…" I couldn't even finish my sentence before she snatched the magazine out of my hands and went on to read it for herself.

I backed away from her because I couldn't believe what I was seeing. My mom, the go with the flow, easy-going, loves everyone, everyone has the best intentions, naïve, easily swayed, kind of person had morphed into this decisive force. Now she was sure of herself no one could sway her of anything.

"$300 per month," she mused, looking up at the ceiling and doing mental math, "That is more than we are paying now but not really, board at Tracy's went up to $150, plus what I pay for shavings, hay, and grain, it is really only $75 more a month, I could pay for that with my hair dressing tips."

This might actually be happening. The wheel was moving, I decided to add to the conversation,

"It said they have an indoor too, so I don't have to stop riding for the winter."

"That's right! You need that! Call them, call them right now and ask if we can tour the place tonight!" She threw the magazine back to me. She ran downstairs and got the phone, pushed the phone button and chucked it at me.

"DIAL!"

I fumbled with the phone and the magazine and got the number in. After two rings, a woman's voice answered,

"Wind Row Equestrian Center this is Helen, how can I help you?"

"Umm, yes, hello, we were interested in finding a new place to board my horse and are wondering if we could tour the facility. Tonight, if possible." I waited, hoping I sounded adult enough to be taken seriously.

"Uh, yeah, sure thing. We have a special event with cows tonight but you can come, what time?"
I looked at my mom and mouthed,

"What time?"

"Seven?" she whispered, but gave me a look as if she wasn't sure herself.

"Seven? "I asked, trying to sound more sure.

"Yeah, sure that is perfect, the cows will be wrapping up then so we will have time to chat, but you can still see them."

"Okay, perfect, see you then, thank you!"

I looked at my mom in disbelief, not sure of what we just did.

"Well, seven it is!" she yelled as she spun on her heel and thundered back down the stairs.

What was happening?

Alex Tyson

The Cowboys

Seven came soon enough and we drove a good fifteen minutes down dirt roads to Wind Row. Mom talked nonstop about how much better and shorter of a drive it was the whole way there. She did quiet down though when we pulled into the driveway, awed at how magnificent the place was.

A large white barn with a green roof was the focal point upon pulling off the road. It was beautiful and huge, 80X200 ft. As we kept driving, you could see another barn, a twin to the first one that was slightly sloped down a hill with a breezeway between them, and a spot where people were clearly parking.

"Okay, this is it!" Mom said as she parked the car and started looking around at the splendor of it all.

This was a huge upgrade from Tracy's. I could already tell Mom was scoping out the cleanliness of everything and was pleased with what she saw. Out of the car and gawking, it wasn't long before we were greeted by Helen, a sharp, no nonsense, shorter lady in her forties. She showed us around the barn, 50 stalls, tack stalls, wash racks, tack rooms for every block of stalls. It was one of the nicest barns I had ever been to. Everything was swept. Mats were in the stalls. There was a horse vacuum. Order. Order.

Nice as it was, that was not what piqued my interest. When we went up into the arena, just like Helen said on the phone, there were cows!

One rider on a paint horse galloped after a rogue black little cow that was running away from the herd and right towards us. The rider urged the paint to go even faster and closer to the cow. The paint had its neck extended forward, nostrils flaring and ears back, his nose was about even with the little cow's hip... then his shoulder, then his nose!

At that, the rider sat back and turned the horse into the cow, wrapping tight to it like a candy wrapper and spinning the cow in the other direction. Wow!

Coming from mostly English barns and background I had never seen anything like it! The skill it must have taken! How brave the horse was! I wanted to learn to ride like that!

As I stood in wonder at what I was seeing, a cowboy came walking towards us. He had a lean build but broad shoulders, wrangler jeans that he wore up high with a belt, square toed cowboy boots, an orange long sleeve button down shirt, and a tan felt cowboy hat. He was handsome, in a defined kind of way, and he looked to be my mom's age. He had laugh lines around his eyes, a handlebar mustache that swooped around into a neatly groomed goatee. He smelled like leather and cologne.

He clearly knew Helen and didn't say hi to her, but he didn't say hi to my mom first either. He walked right up to me.

"Hi there, little Lady! Helen says you are looking for a new place for your horse?"

I looked at my mom, unsure, but she nodded so I carried on

"Yes, Sir. Her name is Pepper, she is a Quarab. And I am Alex."

"Well, nice to meet you" he looked me right in the eye, I don't know if anyone had ever done that before. He saw me, it's like he knew what was going to happen.

He introduced himself to my mom and started walking around with us. He had confidence that drew me to him. You wanted to be around him, he made you feel special. He explained that he was the main trainer here at Wind Row, along with his partner, who was the man riding the paint gelding. Less handsome than The Cowboy, taller, lankier, with darker features and only a mustache, The Quiet One, let's call him, did eventually come over to us, but he remained in the background. The Cowboy always took center stage.

The Cowboy asked me a lot of specific questions about my riding, questions that showed a genuine interest in what I was doing. Questions like:

How long have you been riding?

How long have you had your horse?

What is a big goal you have?

What have you been most proud of in your riding as of right now?

What do you think you need to work on?

We talked for a good twenty minutes. I told him all about how Pepper reared on command, how I liked jumping, that I wanted to keep showing and get better, and how I was good at bareback riding. The cowboy said a lot of things about his experience-he was a nine-time world champion on the Appaloosa Circuit, and he coached a lot of junior riders to high national placings.

If my summer thus far with Pepper had been magic, this was the dream. This was everything I could have ever wanted but never had the words to explain. The Cowboy seemed to understand me in a way the other adults didn't. He sensed I wanted to do a good job, but didn't have all the tools. He promised to show me. I told him about how Pepper acted off the property and he understood! He explained there were ways to stop it! I thought I just had to deal with it, but there was a way forward! I could tell my mom was totally lost, and didn't understand half of the horse language that we were using. The Cowboy did talk to her by herself, presumably about me, when I walked off with Helen to watch the cows being put back in the trailer to go back to the stock owner's house. By the time we left I couldn't contain my joy,

"Mom, we have to be here!"

"I know Alex, I think this was meant to be!" I don't know if she actually knew or believed that, but she definitely saw the wonder in my eyes, how my voice trembled with possibilities, and how The Cowboy knew what to say, and how I felt. Seen, understood, wanted.

We called Helen up the next day to confirm our stall and arrange transport for Pepper.

We had Helen's husband pick Pepper up a few days later when we knew Tracy wouldn't be home. My mom left a note on the board,

PEPPER IS GONE AND WE HAVE LEFT. YOU ARE PAID UP UNTIL THE END OF THE MONTH. I HAVE NEVER BEEN TREATED SO RUDELY IN MY LIFE. GOODBYE.

And just like that, we made the move that would change my life because of compulsive, slightly inconsiderate cleaning.

~*Adult Reflections*~

Wow. There is a lot to unpack here. No matter what, my mom was wrong; not her property, not her stall. When you board somewhere, you are given what is stated in your contract. In our case, we provided all the materials and cleaned the stall, Tracy fed and turned out the horses. One is obligated to do things and use the property as the owner wishes it to be done. Period. If you don't like it, well, you can move. If I ever saw Tracy today, I would apologize. My mom caused damage to the stall and it was going to be a lot of work to relevel it. That was 100% on my mom.

Management-wise, stall mats are better, and if I was in Tracy's position having people clean their own stalls, I would provide mats to avoid this very problem. Mats cut down on shavings, keep the floor from being damaged, and are overall more comfortable for the horse. The initial few hundred dollars of investment will pay for itself within the year.

If I was a barn manager, I don't think I would have left that note on the board. But, in her defense, she did try to tell my mom several times.

I am sure to this day my mom still believes she is right. At the time, as a child, I didn't know what to do and just went along with what my mom was doing.

I never hung out with April and Liz again. I did hear through the grapevine that they both ended up quitting riding. I showed in that same county for years afterwards and never saw them show again.

I do think that God has an interesting sense of humor and often does work out bad situations for good. This situation was ridiculous but it turned into the catalyst that changed my life totally and made me the rider I am today. Meeting The Cowboy and The Quiet One was the best thing that ever happened to me. Through them, I also eventually met my future husband! All because my mom wouldn't listen and just had to clean. Life is weird like that.

Alex Tyson

Ride In the Right Order

      I shake my head whenever I think about my misadventures with Pepper. How naïve and incredibly stupid I was. Of course, it's easy to laugh now because I finally stopped all of my ridiculous behavior.

      To an extent, there has to be room for that in the horse industry. There has to be the opportunity for newcomers to dive in and make mistakes. That's how we learn. That being said, I needed to learn and learn fast. I really should have had adults helping me in this area, but instead I had to learn the hard way until I moved to Wind Row. That's where I finally started to understand how to handle horses outside of the lesson ring, how to deal with disobedient and exuberant behavior, and how to calm an agitated horse, skills that would have helped me avoid some of these circumstances in the first place.

      I see myself in many new riders, and I try to be the person for them that I needed at the time. I developed what I like to call my *Ride in the Right Order* philosophy, which I will expound upon a little bit here. I know that not everyone will agree with me and take my advice. There is always the story of someone who "did it the hard way" and turned out fine. I could even be put into this category to an extent. For that person, congratulations to you. However, it is truthful to point out that for every person that does that, there are probably nine that get seriously injured, or get so scared and overwhelmed they quit. I believe this doesn't need to happen and there is a better philosophy that works for more people. Also, the former method is not so kind to the horse, who surely has an opinion about everything that is happening to them as the person, "just figures it out."

Based on my personal experiences, and what I've observed as a riding instructor: **I firmly believe that beginners need to ride in a supervised situation on a quiet horse until they can master basic riding. When they begin to move on to intermediate riding, more independence can and should be given, but care should be taken to introduce new situations in a supervised way.**

Below are definitions of the above concepts:

What is supervised?

Supervised riding is when there is a person with at least a fair degree of horse knowledge watching the younger and or less experienced person ride. The "supervisor" needs to be able to talk the rider through any issues they may be having, and also be able to handle the horse if need be. This can range from a parent or older sibling who has a good handle on basic riding skills and handling horses, to a trained riding instructor who has studied rider biomechanics and horse behavior.

What is basic riding?

To me, basic or beginner riding is when the rider is not yet capable of walk, trot, and canter, in a balanced fashion, without stirrups.

Why no stirrups?

When you rely on your stirrups for balance, you are constantly thinking about your own balance and self-preservation — making it next to impossible to think about the horse and how to solve any issues the horse may have. This rider is more likely to fall off or pound on their horse's back excessively when they jump or gallop or if the horse moves quickly. The lack of finesse and body awareness also makes these riders poor at movements that require more subtle cues like trail competitions, side passing, and dressage.

Fear in riding also goes away through progressive conditioning. If you know you are balanced in most situations, you are less likely to become nervous, grip the horse with your legs, fall forward, or hold onto the reins with tension, when the horse inevitably spooks or gets nervous. You can rely on your own balance and can just address the situation at hand.

    A foundation in basic riding and mastering your own balance is essential to the lifelong rider. Care should be taken to develop your basic riding seat first, before moving on to really anything else. It takes longer in the beginning, but it is well worth it in the long run. These skills are best cultivated on a quiet school-type horse, who will allow the rider to make all the mistakes that come along with learning.

What is a quiet horse?
    A quiet horse is typically an older horse who has "been there and done that." This horse will have lots of experiences, like going off the property for shows and trail rides, staying in a stall away from home, being away from the herd and riding in a group of horses. The horse usually has smaller, smoother gaits and is easy to handle on the ground. Any horse when handled by inexperienced people can develop bad habits, so the quiet horse must also be schooled occasionally by capable hands. However, the quiet horse is this way, say, 90% of the time, and this is what you want to learn your basic riding on.

What are new situations?
    Only after basic riding is achieved, should the rider try and branch out and handle the horse is situations that are not organized ones designed to succeed. This can include: trail riding, how to handle a horse off the property, how to deal with a nervous horse, how to do a one-rein emergency stop,

riding in a show, etc. I believe that if I could have had an experienced person help me learn how to handle a horse off the property, how to stop a runaway, and other basic safety training, I could have mastered it without as much risk so much more quickly. I doubted my abilities for a long time because of these negative experiences, and that came to be a problem later.

Supervised riding on quiet horses is also critical as a riders transition into the intermediate level for the best chance of success.

What is intermediate riding?

I define intermediate riding as building on your basic riding skills, and broadening your experience with horses. An intermediate rider would be comfortable and competent in new situations, and also be able to ride minor disobediences such as: correctly ride a spook, deal with minor bucks and spins, handling a nervous horse, and learning how to habituate a horse to a scary object/ scenario.

The learning curve:

From my own experience, I had the first part of this equation, but not the second. I learned Walk, trot, canter without stirrups on relatively quiet horses. Had I not had this experience, I know I would have been injured, quit, or both with Pepper. This confidence through basic riding skills was the only thing that allowed me to somewhat stay on and not get into even worse trouble.

As I transitioned into horse ownership, intermediate riding, and new experiences, I needed an experienced person to help me and avoid a lot of pitfalls. Obviously, I didn't have it and thus all the stories. It worked out for me, but I would never put someone in the same situation that I was in.

What it boils down to is: take the time, effort, and energy to befriend, or employ, an experienced person to be in a mentorship role for you while you master basic riding and new situations. You will be ahead in the long run.

Time to Train

My life changed a lot at Wind Row. Quickly, very quickly, I was learning.

I finally got the structure I needed, and I grew exponentially, doubling my abilities in rapid time. The Cowboy didn't give out praise very often, but when he did, he boomed with it. This motivated me to get his approval, and was just the right balance of tough love and encouragement that I needed to grow.

After about two weeks of lessons, I was doing a turn on the haunches, turn on the forehand, neck reining, and side passing, all things I had never done before.

Before long, I learned how to ride Western, and was shocked that I liked it, finding it easy to switch between the two styles of riding.

I rode Pepper bareback all the time at the barn, and seeing how good my seat was, The Cowboy started having me ride some of his younger training horses.

These horses were a little green, and needed someone who could ride bigger gaits and were not easily scared. I don't remember being a natural rider when I started, but I could feel that I was a natural at training. Breaking down everything so the horse could understand was so easy, it made perfect sense. I also loved seeing the light in people's eyes when they saw I could do something that they asked.

The Cowboy gave me the who, what, where, when, why, on everything I needed with whatever horse I was on, and I followed those instructions to the letter. Other people at the barn saw my riding skills and allowed me to exercise their horses, I did this for free at first, but after a while charged $10 a horse and had quite the little side business going.

Helen had ten horses of her own that she let me ride whenever I wanted, and would even give me a project to undertake.

"Teach this one to jump," or, "Take this one out on the trail more so he gets less spooky."

Seeing my potential, The Cowboy let me ride slowly greener and greener horses. Eventually, I got on a big black gelding that had only cantered three times. It took me almost ten uninterrupted minutes of trying to get him to canter, but I never quit, and got him into it eventually.

Upon seeing this, The Cowboy suggested to my mom that we purchase this three-year-old horse, and I could train him up and have a nicer horse to show than we could afford to buy in a year or two.

Many of my new friends at the barn, both adult and kid, tried to talk me out of it, and rightly so. This is not an endeavor most twelve-year-olds should take on.
Starry eyed dreams prevailed and we did buy the horse, and I was successful. Very successful in fact.

While we were only able to show on the local circuit, in a year my gelding, Vador, was winning almost everything in the English and jumping classes.

Because of my success with Vador, I was gifted the opportunity to break one of Helen's horses, Little Q, from scratch.

I was on a rise and I knew it. I was tickled pink with all my opportunities and couldn't believe this was real life.
I almost never made stupid mistakes when working with the baby horses entrusted to me as I appreciated the responsibility.

In this next round of stories, my early ignorance was replaced with antics that fell into two categories: either the natural learning curve of learning to train young horses and show in harder classes, or my belief that the cautionary advice didn't apply to me. Sometimes I considered a lot of things before making a decision, but miscalculated or underestimated one of those variables.

In some ways I was a child prodigy, successfully riding young horses and making a lot of progress.
In other ways I was still a kid, doing dumb things and paying for it.

Making the Judge Laugh

I was about thirteen, guiding Vador around the courtesy circle before the first fence in our course. The first jump of this equitation course was an end jump, a horizontal jump placed just off the rail of the short side of the arena.

Typically, an end jump is toward the middle of the short side, but at this show it was placed a little too close to the corner you had just come out of in your circle. It was a 4H show, and I am fairly confident someone randomly decided the jump should go here, without realizing how difficult this placement was for the 2'6" jumping class. That seemed to happen a lot in 4H jumping classes at the time, but I digress.

I knew that in order to get the right spot to the first fence my horse's stride couldn't be too long or else I wouldn't make the turn. However, I also knew that I needed impulsion and energy to make it up and over the fence, given the short distance from the corner. I would give it three strides. As we got closer to the arc of the circle that would blend into the corner, I knew I had to get Vador over as deeply into the corner as possible to give myself maximum room to turn. I closed my inside leg and outside rein to push him over, while ever so slightly lifting my inside rein to keep his shoulder from dropping in the turn, thus killing our momentum. The sand was deeper than I thought and I could feel Vador getting bogged down.

Go on…go on… go on…

Vador got through the turn and headed straight for his jump. I didn't like the feel of the canter that I had gotten coming out of the turn, sluggish, his energy sucked away by the sand. I tried to keep him moving but I didn't want to make a big move and mess Vador up from his takeoff spot.

Maybe he will chip in a little too close for me and bunny hop over it?

That was becoming more and more like reality as we were two strides away, now one... I closed my leg and... DEAD STOP.

I understood why Vador stopped but it wasn't like him to not even attempt the fence. He usually at least tried. Oh well, the chance for winning the class is out, I thought to myself, and regrouped to finish. You always finish your course or your class, even if you make a huge mistake; it is the unwritten law of horse showing. Leaving the ring in frustration is considered terribly bad form. The only acceptable, and required, reason to leave the ring is if you or your horse fall or the judge asks you to leave.

My mind switched over into training mode instead of competition mode. This was an opportunity to make Vador a braver jumper instead of doing well in the class. Since I had already lost at this point, I would do whatever I needed to get him over the fence.

I took a deep breath to steady myself as I went behind the jump to start another circle. There wasn't a better line or way of travel to the fence, the tight corner was the only option. I decided instead to change *how* I approached the fence. My plan was to go faster through the turn so I could keep my impulsion and momentum, since that seemed to be the problem last time. By doing so I was risking going too fast, and also not making the turn, but I didn't see any other way forward, and I certainly didn't want to make the same mistake twice.

I urged Vador into a bigger canter, lightening my seat and pushing with my legs when his nose extended forward. He was happy to oblige me and picked up a bigger pace, longer, faster, and with more power from his hind end. I decided not to go as far into the corner because that is where the deep sand was.

I picked my eyes up as I guided Vador into the corner, but not right next to the wall and I never sat in my seat to do it. In turn he sliced the corner a little, leaning a bit down with his shoulder. Once we got straight, I corrected the leaning and kept going forward, regaining our pace. We felt a little strung out but I was sure we could make it. Two strides, now one, leg on... and I felt Vador lift his shoulders up to take flight! We did it!

And then he put his front legs back down on the ground, dropped his head down and backed up a good three steps.

I was already in my jumping position when he started to jump, my hands on his mane, my hips bent forward and body closer to his. When he stopped and put his head down, the sudden stop and drop flung me forward right off the front of the saddle, headed over his ears to the ground!

Well, here we go...off at a horse show...how embarrassing!

But all of the sudden, I realized that I had landed astride Vador's neck. I was straddling it with both legs, just in front of his shoulders. When he backed up away from the jump, he picked his head up slightly, and in doing so caught me in the fall, holding me on his neck instead.

We stood there for what felt like forever, stunned as I evaluated the situation. Vador stood tense and alert as he had never had a rider here before. I equally didn't expect to be there and just could not believe that I hadn't fallen.

But now this presented a new problem: how on earth do I get back in the saddle? I didn't want to dismount, because that would be the same as a fall and I wouldn't be able to finish the course. He was going over that jump, no matter what! But his neck was also low enough that it wouldn't be an easy scoot upwards and backwards into the saddle. I would have to scoot up his whole neck before I could hit the shoulders and regain my seat.

Faced with all of these issues and still being stunned of where I ended up, I blurted out rather loudly and certainly by accident,

"WELL, THIS IS INTERESTING!"

I honestly thought I had said it under my breath, and it was meant for me. But I shouted it, and the folks on the sidelines who had gathered around to see the kid fall, and who had moments ago gasped as I was launched from my seat, now erupted in uncontrollable laughter.

Since everyone seemed to be laughing, I glanced over at the judge and her scribe and EVEN THE JUDGE WAS LAUGHING! She tried to cover her mouth with her hand in an attempt to be polite, but I could see her sides heave from a serious chuckle.

Well, might as well go with it. I smiled big and laughed a little too. I mean, it *was funny.*

Determined now to give them something to cheer about, I started to scoot back. I prayed that Vador would just stand still because I was confident, I was sitting on the reins and in no position to control him. I put my hands behind me, grabbed some mane, and started shifting my seat from side and side all the while pulling with my arms and scooting back.

I couldn't go too fast, as a horse's neck is a lot skinnier than you think when you are sitting on it, and it would have been really easy to roll off sideways. To his credit, Vador stood very still and let me tightrope climb backwards. Once I got to his shoulders, I felt instantly more stable, switching my hands to the front of me and pushed myself backward rather quickly into the saddle. Not wanting to press my luck I leaned forward, grabbed my reins and got my stirrups back.

A few hoots and hollers from the crowd, impressed at least with my refusal to give up and get down. I took a little bow and saluted the crowd, which made them chuckle again. I wanted them to know I was going to be a good sport before I got back down to the serious business of jumping this end jump.

Vador was going over it this time! Either that or I truly was falling off. I gathered myself, resolved to go, and set on a repeat of the previous tactic. Forward, a little faster, only this time I would take my crop (which somehow in this scenario I didn't let go of) and reach it behind me to give him a good tap on the belly one stride out.

We turned our corner a little more balanced this time and headed straight, two strides out... more leg, one stride, more leg, takeoff... lean forward, one hand back and smack with the stick behind my leg... up and over!
More cheers from the crowd!

I went on to finish the course and of course didn't place, but no matter. I was quite proud of the fact that I got him over that end jump, because it took just about all I had to get over it.

The judge laughed! I thought to myself as I finished the course with a smile on my face.
You don't see that every day!

~Adult Reflections~

I firmly believe that this experience was bestowed upon me for the future riders that I would teach, and then teach to show. Between my own lesson program and my work as a middle school equestrian team coach, I have now guided countless people through their first show.

So many people are nervous. Everyone wants to do a good job, and be the star of the day. Or, at the very least, not embarrass themselves. Since there is a decent chance that the first show won't end with fame and glory, and may include some embarrassment, this little tale is a great icebreaker.

"Even if it doesn't go well, it can't be as bad as what happened to me!"

Even if you do embarrass yourself, it's okay. As with falling off a horse, and a lot of things in life really, if you're not seriously hurt, laugh about it, even if it is at your own expense. And know that everyone else there has experienced — or will — something equally embarrassing at a show!

Vador and I jumping at a show circa 2007.

Buck, Jump, Rear Day

Helen gave me an opportunity.

I was to start Helen's horse, Little Q, under saddle. Completely from scratch. I would be the first one to ride her; like an astronaut on the moon, going where no one had gone before.

Helen had seen my work with Vador, as well as some catch rides on The Cowboy's training horses. She liked what she saw and came up with a pretty fair deal: she wouldn't have to pay to train the horse, and I would get the opportunity to break one from scratch. The plan was for me to barrel race Q (once I figured out how to do that) and Helen wanted me to show Q as I had done with Vador. The Quiet One said he would help me. As far as I know, no one paid him, I know my mom certainly didn't, since we could barely afford what we were already doing.

I knew this was my big chance. I'd get to do something that no one gets to do. The only other people I know that broke horses as young as I was (thirteen at the time) were people who grew up on farms and ranches, and their parents trained horses themselves. A kid who shouldn't have horses to begin with, given the opportunity to train someone else's horse, and have professional help every step of the way to make sure it was right?

How was this my life? I knew this was something sacred, something to hold in my heart and cherish. This was the beginning of everything, I just knew it.

For as many dumb things I did only a few years before, I was now confident from training, riding, and showing

Vador. The Cowboy taught me a lot about horse behavior and training, letting me ride young training horses that were sent to him to start under saddle. He would give me a task, for instance, a turn on the haunches, seat stops, or canter departs, and he would teach me how to teach the horse.

If I had a young one, I knew it was my responsibility to ride and teach them well. I took it 1000% seriously and I never took a short cut. I relished in the responsibility, elated I was worthy enough to work with these horses.

Starting horses is a tedious, slow process that doesn't excite much in the retelling, but is quite exciting when you are doing it, if you have the right attitude.

I broke down every little thing into dozens of smaller pieces, making sure Q was okay with each of them before moving onto the next step. A good mantra for starting young horses is: ask little, expect little or nothing, reward generously.

For example, to mount up from the ground you put your foot in the stirrup, jump up and down to gather momentum, heave yourself over the horse's back, and sit down gently. In order to do this, the horse needs to accept you jumping around them, weight in the stirrups, weight over their back, the sight of a rider on their back, and the look and feel of a person astride. These criteria can be broken down into smaller steps still: weight in stirrup, pushing weight in stirrup, jump up and down pushing weight in stirrup, foot in stirrup, jumping up and down with foot in stirrup, hopping upward a foot, two feet, three feet and hover above them, lay on their back so they can feel the weight, flex their head side to side so they can see you, and finally, sit down. All from both sides as well.

Things are done in this slow, methodical manner with all aspects of the starting process: lunging, accepting the saddle and bridle, going forward with voice cues, stopping with voice cues, mounting, yielding to pressure, and so on.

The first ride should be easy, drama-free, and pleasant for the horse. Which it was for Q. In fact, all of her ground work training, along with the first two weeks of riding were uneventful. We stayed in the round pen (a high walled, metal circle about 60 feet across) and I worked her every day. The Quiet One perched on those high rails watching me. Everything was an easy, upward progression, we had walk, trot, canter both directions, a good stop, and decent turning. There is not much you can do in a round pen after that; it was time to start riding her in the arena.

"Now, I want you to be in here when no one else is for like a week," The Quiet One explained,

"Your goal is to canter and trot for longer, as well as make some big circles around and be able to stop from the trot and canter."

By the end of the week this task was accomplished, and The Quiet One worked a horse with me to have Q get used to another horse moving around the arena as well.

"Okay, this is just what we want," he praised, a rarity,

"Now what you need to do is have wet saddle pads."

I gave him a puzzled look as I had never heard the expression.

"Huh?"

"Wet saddle pads," The Quiet One repeated himself, and seeing no comprehension in my face he continued,

"Time in the saddle. Ride the horse enough to work up a sweat. Wet saddle pads."

I am still not sure I got exactly what he meant. I was riding the horse everyday already.

"Just ride around and start doing more things with her. Ride with other people. Take her for a lap around the barn, ride in lessons with others, ya know?"

That sounded fun, take the training wheels off a bit.

"Every time you come across something new, take the same approach that you have been taking, break it down and introduce it and you should be fine."

That sounded nice, he trusted that I wouldn't be brash and irrational. I could do that.

"Sounds good," I replied simply.

But... well...it turned out not to be that simple.

Taking the training wheels off turned into taking the handlebars off too, and the brakes.

Riding around with The Quiet One was one thing, riding around with an arena full of people was another thing entirely.

It didn't start that way. The first half a dozen or so times Q behaved herself quite well. But then all the problems started all at once.

If someone opened the door suddenly, Q would bolt. If someone moved the barrels around the arena, she would bolt. If someone got too close to her passing her in the arena, she would try to kick.

Windy out? A good day to buck.

See something scary in the far end of the arena? Rear and spin away from it.

EVERY. SINGLE. DAY.

I had started breaking Q at the end of summer, right before school began. Things went well until about October, when the darkness was falling much earlier in Michigan, the wind picked up, and the cold set it. We were confined to that indoor arena. All winter. And all winter this went on.
The Cowboy had taken over much of my training at this point, especially in lessons. The Quiet One helped me out during the week. Rearing, bucking, bolting, shying, one of these happened every day. Sometimes all of them.

I'd been through all of this before (especially rearing, because of Pepper) but I was always a passive rider in these situations. Things just happened and you either stayed on or you didn't. Horse bolted? Hold on until they stopped. Horse bucked? Decent chance you are coming off unless you manage to sit it. Rearing? Well, to me rearing used to be fun, but Q brought this nervous, bolstering energy to it. The controlled lift into the air was replaced with a rocket that spun upward, possibly nearing vertical. A vertical rear was the only rear I was scared of, and Q came awfully close, I felt her hindquarters sway underneath her a few times. All I could do was I clutch her mane, hold still, and pray that we wouldn't tip over.

I could no longer be a passive rider. I was now expected to correct these behaviors. I had to make them stop. But I couldn't make them stop, and I was so, so scared. Her early good behavior had lulled me into a false sense of security and when she inevitably did do a little spook and buck in the big arena, I was unprepared to handle it.

Things spiraled. Tension begat tension. I was scared of her, and she was scared of all my built-up tension and my inability to be confident leader. I needed to take charge and be calm but I just couldn't do it. I was riding on the edge. I began to think this is not for me. I could stay calm on my own, but this was an explosion of nervous energy, and I was barely staying on every time. How on earth could I be calm? We were a kettle on the stove, about to boil over. Something needed to give, but nothing did.

I did however, show up every day, I kept going. I shook a little as I saddled Q up but I always got on. I didn't want to, but I was committed, I'd told Helen I would do this for her. I tried to listen to everything that The Cowboy and The Quiet One said. I managed to stay on, barely, especially with the bucks. Those bucks knocked me forward and out of my seat every time, forcing my hands to catch me so my face didn't plant into her neck. I kept going, but I never really improved.

There was a coffee table book in the observation arena for people to thumb through as they watched lessons. I can't remember the name of it, but it was basically a bunch of inspirational quotes that applied to horseback riding, coupled with some epic picture of a horse to complement each quote. One day, while waiting for my mom to pick me up, I sat in the observation area (which was one of the only places to get warm with its little space heater). I was watching one of The Cowboy's lessons and absent-mindedly flipping through the book when I came across a quote from a name I had heard before, John Wayne. I think he used to be in some old movies my dad watched. The quote?

"Courage is being scared to death, but saddling up anyway."

I did a little chuckle because as soon as I read it, I thought to myself: that's me!

I took to using the saying. While I was literally saddling Q up for what would hopefully not be another buck, jump, rear day, I said under my breath so only Q could hear,

"Courage is being scared to death... and saddling up anyway."

I don't know why, but I almost always seem to stubbornly continue, even when I am miserable. I am a glutton for punishment, convinced that this is just the way it is, I resign myself to misery. Sometimes it's a curse; other times it's a blessing. I carry on far longer than any sane, rational person would. In the process, I learn more than the sane person, and experience more too. Being a little crazy isn't always bad, especially when breaking young horses. At least, that's what I told myself anyway.

But the crazy was about to come to a head. The kettle was about to boil over, and I would soon find out exactly what I was made of, one cold, icy, end-of-February day.

Q and I in her early days of training in the round pen.

Alex Tyson

Thanks, John Wayne

The misadventure started where many horse fiascos do: a windy day.

It was the end of February, typically home to some of the coldest temperatures all year in Michigan. The wind was howling, it was barely twenty degrees out (*before* windchill), and there was ice all over the farm. This made getting horses to and from the fields difficult. The horses too, couldn't move around as much in their field, and as such stayed in the same spot as the hay was. Exercise-wise this is not so different than the horse being locked in the stall. So, when a horse who can't move around reaches the good arena footing, they are far more interested in running around and releasing their pent-up energy than having an enjoyable ride. A good lunge before can help with this problem, which I did every time I rode Q anyway. This day I expected her to be high as a kite, rearing with the wind as it whipped, but she wasn't. She was calmer than normal, actually.

There were five or six people in the arena, so I made sure to stay away from them as much as possible to avoid someone being the accidental victim of Q's shenanigans. People had already gotten the memo I was a little tricky to ride with, so they kept their distance as well.

All in all, it was a pretty easy day, and I was even a little caught off guard at how easy it was. I had walked around for a bit with no spooks, and in the absence of drama, started trotting some circles. Q was a little high headed and trotted off a bit quicker than I expected, but it wasn't too big of a deal. We trotted for a good ten minutes, five or so each way, before I decided we should pick up the canter. More confident than normal, but not totally at ease, I headed over to the far end of the ring, away from the entry door. It looked like people were congregating to leave the ring, being farther away from the crowd is always better on potentially explosive Q, so I moved myself away.

At the far end, seemingly a hazard to no one, I waited until we hit the corner, to help me get the correct canter lead. We got our lead and started a canter circle. We only made it as far as the center of the arena when all hell broke loose.

The wind didn't blow, no one opened the door, nothing had happened; but, nevertheless, we were going up. Q's mane neared my face and I leaned forward as I had done hundreds of times to stay with her in the rear. I made plans to spin her in a circle to the left, away from the direction of the other horses, once we went down. But we didn't go down. In fact, we leaped forward. Q, front feet in the air, pushed her hind legs out behind her and sent all four feet off the ground, propelling us forward and up, like one of the caprioles I had seen the Lipizzaner stallions do at a show. We sailed through the air with superhero like athleticism and I swear I could hear people gasp.

Well, that is always comforting.

At least I was putting on a show.

I wasn't sure how I should land in this situation. Stay forward or lean back? I had reared hundreds of times, I had even leapt like this a little bit, but not a full rear into a leap. I decided that I should lean back as I felt her come down, because it was unlikely she would land on her back legs.

When we finally did land, I was right, she had all four feet on the ground, but I was wrong because she immediately went back up, this time spinning a bit in the air as she did. I made a huge grab forward to avoid the cardinal sin of pulling back in a rear. I practically was laying on her neck to avoid getting left behind. We landed again and I thought she was going to go back up so I stayed slightly forward to avoid making a big move again to stay balanced.

But I was wrong. Now came the bucks.

Q started pitching as hard as she ever had. Buck, buck, buck, buck, buck, no rest, no catching her breath in this athletic endeavor.

After about buck number three I found myself tossed over the front of the saddle and over the saddle horn onto the mare's neck. I instinctively clamped my legs down tight around her neck to avoid slipping off either side. My hands, having lost the reins during my ejection from the seat, were free to grab the mane and try and ride this out. I considered for a split second just giving up and accepting the fall, but she as bucking so hard I feared that she would step on me, or kick me in the head. I had not known this intensity from her before, or any horse for that matter.

By some miracle I stayed on. Frustrated at her inability to get me off with bucks, Q turned her attention to flinging her neck more and bucking less. In the buck her head went up and down, now she was swinging it side to side, and throwing in a circle spin every now in then in an increasingly angry attempt to whip me off.

It is helpless being in this position; there is nothing you can do to improve, influence, or stop the situation. I clamped by legs as tight as I could, braced my arms to keep me in the middle of her skinny neck, and prayed for it to stop.
I held on. I couldn't do anything but that.

Eventually, Q took a brief pause between head tosses to catch her breath. Fate gave me an opportunity, and I vaulted off, swinging my right leg over her neck and hopping awkwardly on my left one as I hobbled away from her. She turned to face me and gave me the stink eye once I was free. I didn't have time to process much because I heard a voice booming from the other end of the arena,

"LUNGE THAT HORSE UNTIL SHE IS DRIPPING WITH SWEAT RIGHT NOW!" Ironically, it was The Quiet One who commanded this.

Sheepishly, I took Q and lead her over to the lunge line, took off her bridle, slipped a halter on, and sent her out in a circle away from me. As soon as I asked her to go away, she kicked out at me, to which I took the lunge whip and cracked her in the hip, sending her more forward. She didn't kick anymore. But she did run. And run. And run. And run. I didn't need to run her until she was dripping with sweat, she did that on her own. When she finally calmed down enough to turn her around, she took off again in the new direction, although this time she didn't try to kick me. Finally, when she brought herself down to a trot I heard The Quiet One boom again,

"NOW PUT A COOLER ON THAT THING AND WALK HER OUT!"

I grabbed a cooler (a fleece blanket used to wick off sweat of hot horses in the winter) stripped off her tack, put the fleece around Q, snugging it up close to her neck that had developed cowlicks from all the sweat. In fact, the whole horse was steaming. She looked like when water is poured over a hot skillet, the steam just billowing into the air. Her sides were heaving from all of the effort that she had just put into running herself ragged.

I walked Q out in silence. No one asked me if I was all right. People just saw this kid trying to ride this young mare that always cleaned her clock and was now doing the walk of shame. I wasn't able to complete my ride, Q hadn't really learned anything from this experience, and I learned that I might be done. This is the stuff that real cowboys do. I am just a girl. Just a kid. I can't do this kind of thing and it isn't for me. Saying that now would be incredibly shameful too, so I wasn't going to announce my decision today. I would later, another day, with no emotion, like The Quiet One would prefer. I had a feeling people would just make fun of me if I said that now.

"Cowgirl up," they would say.

Well, see that is the problem, I thought to myself. *I am no cowgirl. I am just a scared girl.*

Head down, dreams dashed, I went to leave the arena when The Quiet One shouted out a little encouragement, or maybe just a little chuckle on his behalf,

"Well, at least you didn't fall off!"

I didn't think much of it. Sure, I didn't fall off but I had a terrible, terrible time of it. I was petrified, and I had spent my whole evening on this. Between the ride, lunging, and walking out, we were approaching the three-hour mark. My mom would be here soon and the day was shot.

"Yeah," I said flatly as I left, closing the door behind me.

Leading Q into her stall, I grabbed a curry comb. She was dry underneath but a little crusty; I'd need the comb to brush out her crusted hair. Once in her stall Q headed straight for the water, and downed the whole bucket. I left her there and filled another one for her. That one downed as well. Once more to fill up and she just played with this one, splashing her lips around by dunking her head in and out.

Once she was done playing, she just took in a deep, slow, breath and then sighed. It was a tired sigh: she was done. But instead of going right for the hay Q looked at me and put her head toward me, resting her velvet muzzle in my hands. She puffed her exhaling breath into my hands in a slow rhythmic fashion. Slowing down with every breath, and pushing the weight of her head into my hands.

Somewhere I had read that a Native American tribe used to put their head by the nostril of their horse and breathe in their breath, inhaling what they exhaled. They would time it so that when the horse inhaled it was now breathing their human breath, breathing each other in. Breathing in scent, emotions, intention, will. This was supposed to bond them to their horse. As they were doing this, they could call their horse by a secret name that only they knew.

I don't know why I did it, but I crouched down to where Q was resting her muzzle in my hands, and put my face near hers. This didn't seem to upset her, so I pressed my head into her muzzle and looked her in the eyes. Her eyes were a little concerned, but not wary. I breathed her in, the sweet smell of oats, hay, and a little dirt. There was so much breath my lungs filled quickly; it was hard to take it all in. When it was her turn to breath in me, I made sure my breath was long and slow so as not to startle her, but sustained, even.

I am not sure what she must have smelled, I eat a lot of apples and granola bars, so I hoped it smelled a bit like her. Her eyes brightened with my breath and I felt a small tug away, but I gently stoked my fingers on her chin, and sent my energy down into my chest, easy, waiting.

No babe... we are together.

Soon it was my turn again and she leaned a bit more into my hands, relaxing. It was easy for her to give. When she took my breath again this time, she didn't lean into me more, but did not pull away either.

And that's how we came to understand each other.

I am not sure that I realized this when it was happening, I just wanted Q to relax and be with me, I just wanted to be understood and to understand. But I did understand that she did not hate me, nor was she out to get me. Something was just missing.

When I finally got up and I walked away, I was sad to leave. Q lifted her head and watched me go, a little disappointed to be alone now.

I didn't sleep well that night. Did what happened in the stall mean anything? Or was that just me being starry eyed again?

I was actually so perplexed by all of the events that I didn't go to the barn the next day, which was completely unlike me. I wanted to quit with Q. I was scared and way in over my head but I couldn't shake that the answer was there. The Quiet One and The Cowboy had been helping me and nothing too bad had happened, even though I wasn't improving. I hadn't fallen off yet.

Wait.

That was it!

I HADN'T FALLEN OFF YET!

I had just experienced the worst ride of my life! The top end of my abilities, and I HADN'T FALLEN OFF. Q had bucked, reared, bolted, all of the above, one right after another, EVERY SINGLE DAY AND I HADN'T FALLEN OFF.

That was it. I needed to stop being afraid. I needed to stop worrying about what Q would do because whatever she would do, I could ride it. I hadn't fallen off. I was better than I thought. I just needed to act like it.

I needed to ride more confidently when Q did her antics and stop acting like a victim. I wasn't going to fall. I could ride it.

I could ride it.

I came the next day and didn't shake while I tacked up, although I did quote John Wayne, a little louder this time. Q spooked in the corner almost immediately when I got to walking around, I easily turned her into the imaginary monster on the wall and chuckled,

"Nothing there silly, walk on!"

I ignored her completely and sent her forward, steady reins and leg on, she still looked at the monster a little but obliged.

Another spook happened when the door opened, only this time she scooted forward, raising her head high in the air. I let her go for a step and just said,

"Hey there, easy," with a light lift on the reins. Q came back to a hurried trot and I passed the lady entering the arena and said to her,

"A little frisky today I guess?" and carried on.

The canter transition led to a few crow-hops (small bunny hop bucks) after the first stride,

"Ahh! Ahh!" I firmly said and gave her a little kick, sitting back, and raising my arms up in a little jerk every time she tried.

It was different this time. Not frantic. I used the minimum amount of pressure to get her to keep her head up and go forward.

Hopeful at my discovery, the next day I only had two spooks. Then a little buck in the simple change the next day.

Little by little Q changed for the better, because I did first. She needed me to be steady, be there for her. I was in the beginning, but I needed to learn to do it when she was scared first. I was good at creating an environment where she wasn't scared in the first place. But then, when more things happened that were out of my control, I had to control myself despite what Q might be doing and help her out of it. I was too worried about myself and my own balance to do that.

For the rest of the time that I got to ride and train Q, she was a pretty steady horse. She stopped all her bad habits.

And I never, ever, fell off her.

-Adult Reflections-

This was a turning point, not just at the time, but also for my riding career. No doubt, Q's protests would have gotten louder and louder, resulting in more blowups. Now, as a riding instructor, the takeaway is this:

1. If you are having explosions there is almost always a reason, and it's more than likely the reason is you.

2. Get help with how to ride these things if they are happening. I had that and still had trouble. I can't imagine trying to do it on one's own--it would be next to impossible.
3. Training horses requires taking on a certain amount of risk, more than typical riding. It is not if, it's when, an injury will happen. Anyone interested in this must accept this or not do it in the first place.

It can be very, very, easy to become afraid. I am convinced the antidote to fear is realizing not that what you are afraid of will stop-because it probably won't-but instead that you can handle it. This was without a doubt one of the hardest times in my riding career. If I had quit then, I would have never continued and learned what I needed to learn to become a trainer.

I had listened to The Quiet One and done everything I was supposed to in Q's early days, setting a good foundation. But the middle was challenging. I expected Q to never do anything "bad" because I had followed the rules. Sometimes that happens and the horse almost never puts a toe out of line. Vador was like that, he hardly ever did anything "bad," ever.

Because my previous experience was with a well-behaved horse, I was shocked when Q was so different. That shock came across as nervousness which just added fuel to the fire. I was so scared that I didn't see I was causing more problems than I was helping with. That horse needed me to be there for her and I let her down and caused her to be afraid, looking for more and more things to defend herself against because I was no help.

But when I realized that I could ride it, that I could handle everything that came at me, my attitude changed and I started being a better leader for her. Mental abilities came after physical ones.

Alex Tyson

Over the Hill and Through the Woods

Once it was confirmed I was no longer a menace to society, The Quiet One allowed me to participate group barrel lessons.

I started learning barrels, and teaching Q to do barrels, simply because Helen wanted me to. At the time I rode pretty much exclusively English and did equitation and jumping classes with Vador. I had no real interest in barrels at first, but I was always willing to give anything a try, to learn.

I discovered it was fun to whip around those turns, there was a lot more to it than I thought. It was all about getting the horse to bend his body around the barrel so he could keep driving with his hindlegs, tight and fast, without losing momentum. It was a real challenge to keep track of — where was the nose? The ribs? The hind end? Is everything in alignment?

I learned about indirect reining and leg yields, a new skill which I realized was a dressage skill as well.

"Barrel racing is basically dressage at thirty miles an hour," The Cowboy would say. I didn't really understand that at the time, but I did understand it wasn't just whip and spur. There was a lot of finesse to this.

Another unique aspect to learning barrels was that initially I knew nothing about it, and obviously Q didn't know how to run and turn barrels either. The saying usually goes, *green and green makes black and blue,* meaning an inexperienced rider plus and inexperienced horse results in everyone getting hurt. This is certainly true for breaking young horses, introducing horses to new situations, jumping, and almost anything new to a horse.

In most scenarios, you must be significantly more experienced than the horse to even attempt teaching it. Absent this, you risk messing up your horse, possibly beyond repair, and it is highly likely you'll wreck yourself as well.

I quickly found that the old saying did not hold true in barrels. Since the horses are learning how to turn and then eventually run, they don't know right away that they are supposed to go fast. The rider can't go that fast either so, well, no one goes fast. Horse and rider gain in accuracy and confidence, and then the speed comes. For barrels, it would almost be worse to put an inexperienced person on a fast, automatic horse because the rider would most likely end up in the dirt, being out run and out-turned by the horse that knows what it's doing. Now, granted, this only holds true if the rider was experienced at riding, and the horse was already decently trained to ride before starting this barrel racing journey together, but it is still an interesting phenomenon.

~

As our training progressed, it became apparent that Q had weak stifles. A stifle on a horse is anatomically similar to a knee on a person, but is located up in the hip by their flank. The stifle has a cool locking mechanism that allows a horse to sleep standing up.

But if the mechanism isn't working properly, the stifle can get "stuck" in one position and the horse is forced to drag their leg out behind them. Or the horse will refuse to move at all. When the stifle is stuck, backing up can help unlock it, and you can sometimes see and hear when it happens, but it isn't a good long-term solution.

Long term you need to build up the hind end by trotting over poles and hills. Sometimes weak stifles happen because of the way the horse is "built," and sometimes it's due to an injury...but whatever the reason, it seriously hinders a horse's athletic career. In many cases it can be helped but is aways something to be mindful of. I have heard of people doing surgery, but that was not discussed with Q.

At any rate, once we discovered that her stifle was locking up when her work load increased, I was tasked with building that hind end by working her on the various hills that we had out back.

Wind Row's property had a strange layout. The barn was in the center, with a driveway that circled all the way around it. The pastures were laid out in a circle surrounding the barn, so it was never too far of a walk to enter any particular field. Past the fields was a patch of woods that eventually lead to a set of train tracks. On the other side of the tracks, the path lead past a huge manure spreading field, and then to a private lake, which sadly was too mucky and narrow to swim horses in. Just off to the side of the lake was an absolutely massive hill mostly made of sand. You could tell at one point an excavator had dug into the sand, cutting away the hill so it resembled more of a cliff. There was a steep wooded path that went up the side on an angle, and when you walked over to the sand cliff, you could see the field and the lake from your vantage point.

The wooded trail that went up to the cliff climbed through the woods before crossing the plateau of the cliff, then looping back around to that same wooded path. My friends and I often rode at least to the railroad tracks and back to cool our horses out, although a few times a week we would either go to the woods or around the manure field. The train tracks butted right up to the back of many of the pastures and least one train passed through a day. The horses were pretty indifferent to the train when they were out in their pastures, but it was a different story when the train is hurtling right in front of you, or you get stuck on the other side of the tracks as the train goes by.

This of course never stopped us; we just were very careful to listen for trains.

"Go trot her around all those hills back there, maybe even work up to walking up that big sand thing like *The Man from Snowy River*," The Cowboy told me. I had no idea where Snowy River is or who the man was, but I put together that it was a movie and there was a big ledge involved. I had seen the Cowboy go down the sand cliff himself with a horse before, the sand swooshing away from his feet as he did, his head almost touching the horse's hindquarters, shoving his hand forward so his mount could drop his head and see where its feet were. The horse had slowly descended down the hill and picked its way through as it sunk and slid a little with every step down.

I had no desire to go down or up that hill. Seemed dangerous.

But, as I went back there every day to trot in the wooded hills alongside the sand cliff, I began to eye it more and more, looking for a spot where I could climb up or down it. While studying it, I realized that those who traversed it (mainly The Cowboy and The Quiet One) used routes that were off to the side of the hill, and followed a natural crevasse in the sand. It wasn't straight up; it was up on a sharp angle. As the days passed and as Q seemed to be getting stronger, I noticed one path up to the side that was shorter than the others. It was fairly straight up, but it didn't seem vertical and it would put me on the far side of the sand cliff, where the exit seemed flatter and sloping. I examined from the upside of the trail on the plateau as well, it was pretty straight up for about eight feet, then it tapered to the edge, decently flat, as opposed to straight up for twenty feet and a ninety-degree angle for a ledge more in the middle of the cliff in most other spots.

I wasn't stupid, and I waited until I was going up there with some friends to try to go up the sand cliff. I didn't however, tell them what my plans were, which didn't really matter because they couldn't help me anyway. I just wanted them around in case I fell off for some reason. I had been up plenty of hills at this point and I knew the drill: stay in the middle of the saddle but rise up out of your stirrups, sink the weight into your heels, bend your hip forward and put your hands halfway up the neck, eyes up and through the ears to where you are going. This allowed me to stay balanced and the horse to use its hind end to push up the hill while its head and neck were free to see where it was going and could swing it to adjust its balance. The only thing to me that was different about the sand cliff was the sand, which I knew meant Q would need to keep moving so she wouldn't get bogged down in it, unable to climb.

I approached my intended path nice and straight at a brisk walk, once we got to where Q needed to pick her shoulders up and start climbing, I got into my forward position and gave her a little squeeze with both legs, asking her to keep her momentum. Q responded and pushed with her legs, jutting her jaw forward and lengthening her neck to keep her weight out in front of her. After just a few steps Q seemed to get really into it and I could tell her pushing legs had changed from a quick walk to a little trot.

Typically, you want your horse to walk up a hill for control's sake, but I didn't want to pull back or tell her to slow down in this terrain either, so I let it go, figuring she knew better how to balance herself than I did. Everything was going well until I noticed that we were getting a little off the path, drifting more into the center of the sand cliff, where it was steeper and the sand not as packed down. I touched my right leg to Q, asking her to move over, and opened my left rein slightly, just enough to suggest but not enough to knock her off balance.

Q tried to oblige, but then I felt her hip slip out from under her. Her right leg started to sink, deep and down clear past her hock and her left hind leg scrambled diagonally out to the side, trying to find purchase. She splayed her front legs wide, trying to get a better gripping stance as her hip started to sway to the right towards the center of the sand cliff. It almost felt like she was doing the splits.

Not good… but just stay here.

I waited it out, hoping Q would right herself and stand back up.

But she didn't. I felt her rock backward instead.

Her front legs start to lighten and lean back, her head was even coming back toward me, instead of lurching down and forward to get more grip. The hind end started to shake and wobble, losing grip and resolve.
We were going to go backwards, flip over, and spin down the hill.

I absolutely was NOT DOING that, so I kicked my feet out of the stirrups and looked for an escape route. With the way we were leaning, I couldn't get off to the right because I would get rolled over on, but the left was getting higher and higher with every passing moment, and I doubted I could leap over that side and clear her legs.
With no time left I decided to go full western and get Q up that cliff.

I threw my body forward on her neck to get some more weight on the front legs, put my hand just about to her ears and hissed,

"GEEEEEEEEEETTTTTTTTT GET!" I kicked wildly as if my life depended on it, because, it kind of did.

Q was able to be in neutral for a moment, neither continuing to flip back but not going forward.
I took this as proof that what I was doing was working and carried on even more,

"GET! GET! GET! GET UP! GO ON!"

Q made a big move and swung her neck to the left, getting her legs under herself and standing upright.

Yes! She is up! No, go on!

"THAT'S IT! UP! UP!"

Q plunged her neck forward and got her legs moving, small movements, but she chugged forward as if a struggling train.

Up...up... up...

The terrain got steeper as we went and I kept my leg on, encouraging Q with every step, although not as frantic as I was before she got back up. We chugged our way up to the top. Once we were clear and over the ledge I fell on Q's neck and gave her a hug.

"Thank you," I whispered to her. She stood still, her neck bouncing up and down from her heaving, labored breaths from climbing this sand pit.

My friends, who were still at the bottom yelled up to me in astonishment,

"ARE YOU NUTS?"

"Botched stifle practice!" I called back. I don't think they really knew what I was doing, or rather attempting to do. It was, indeed, botched.

They made their way up, although not via the cliff, and we finished our loop around the woods. I did, however, elect to go down via the sand cliff on the same path. After riding up it, I knew down would actually be pretty easy.

I was right. Q slowly picked her way through, nose down to the sand, sinking a little with each step in the front, and sliding a little in the back, but carefully inching on to the next step, slow and deliberate. My friends didn't try the down trek but did watch me come down it in case I had a wreck like the first time. But no, easy. To this day I think down is a little safer than up, as long as your horse is slow and careful.

My friends totally did tell on me, and there was still a significant sand mark on Q's hip as evidence of our near flip.

The Cowboy just laughed. People tended to do that if nothing bad or lasting happened. Just laugh and go onto the next thing. In general, I think that is good advice, but it helps if you learned something while laughing. Which I guess I did, because I never went up that hill again on Q, only down. I did take Vador up it a few times without incident, his powerful hips pushing through the sand as if it were nothing.

Years later at CHA certification camp, we all got together in one of the girl's cabins and watched *The Man from Snowy River*, which is a good movie, and I get the comparison. But his hill was down, way, way down. I was a little disappointed at that, given my own experience. I will give it to him, though, he definitely rode it better.

-*Adult Reflections*-

When I think of this story, I can't help but think: "Right idea, wrong execution."

I tried to do what was right by going up and down hills. I tried to prepare by going up and down lots of hills before I tried the sand cliff. I had watched people go up the sand cliff, and I had done a lot of hills myself, so my route picking and technique were correct. Really, this is just missing one detail: the horse had bad stifles. Because of this, Q was more predisposed than most horses to have a hard time in the deep sand (which puts extra pressure on the stifle) and the steep hill (more pressure still). While most of what I did was well thought out, I was asking too much of that individual horse, especially at that time in her development.

Emergency Dismount

When I was at horse camp at Haverhill one year, way before I got Pepper, they made us fall off on purpose. This is about as scary as it sounds, at least at first. A helper walked alongside the horse, keeping them straight at the walk; we were instructed to slip off, keep our head up, not break our fall with our arms, hit the ground and roll away from the horse. Everyone's eyes were as big as saucers when we were given this lesson plan for the day.

"Now I know what you're thinking," the instructor started, "but this is one of the best things you can do for your riding, if you can fall right, you are less likely to get seriously hurt. If you are not seriously hurt you can ride more, and for longer."

That sounded pretty good to me. Everyone my age had heard of a famous actor who was paralyzed from a terrible horse jumping accident. I had seen people break bones and get in nasty wrecks. I knew freak things happened even if people did everything correctly. Learning to fall wasn't a guarantee to ride forever, but it might help. I resolved to do it. I don't think I had much of a choice, but I made peace with it in my head at least.

Making yourself fall is an interesting business. You must surrender to fear, the unknown, and potential pain, willingly. There is a very tense moment right before you decide to let go and a very panicked moment after you do. But, following instructions, landing on my side and rolling away; I was surprised how little it hurt to fall in the big, deep, sandy arena. I was basically landing on a pillow.

Once we had done it a few times at the walk it was time to do it at the trot.

"Now, I want you to feel the rhythm of the horse. You know up, down, up down at the trot?"

We nodded, standing in a circle, waiting to be led off again to our fate. I could tell the other girls wanted her to keep talking so they could delay falling again.

"If possible, try to slip off on the down step with the inside shoulder, when it comes back towards you. You won't have so much momentum in the fall. If you don't think you can push yourself away from the horse, the ups step will be better because you will have that momentum."

I was a little concerned about propelling myself far enough from the horse's hooves and decided to try and time my fall with the leg that would give me a little boost off.

Before we knew it, we were off, well, people started to go off. A helper would hold the horse and trot them down the long side of the arena, and the student would fall off to the inside (towards the middle of the arena) with the instructor watching close by. Once they were up and out of the way, another helper rotated in and took the next horse. Watching people fall was a little terrifying, I knew what was in store for me. I watched as people slipped awkwardly, landing too hard, not keeping their head up, not rolling and slamming down, splat, like a pancake.

I didn't see anyone doing it right, so I catalogued a lot of what not to do. Soon enough, it was my turn and I was being led away to the gallows.

One, two, one, two, one, two... I counted the rhythm and tried to look for the shoulder to time my decent at the right time. This was extraordinary difficult, and too much information to give us kids really because when you are fighting your mind to let go and plummet downward, off of a moving 1,000 lb. animal, you would have to be 100% confident doing it to feel the timing. I tried my best but I had no clue what step I was on.

I did figure out fast that the ground came up quicker, I had to make a quick move keeping my head up, the impact was almost softer then at the walk, and the roll away easier because I had more energy to work with. I rose a little shaken, but felt surprisingly good.

"Good job! Just like that!" the instructor said. At least I could be good at falling. Following this exercise I felt a lot more relaxed falling, which I suppose was the point. Even if you don't fall correctly, if you are relaxed, you are less likely to get hurt. In times since I have often been told I was a "graceful faller." Graceful is not a word I would use to describe myself, ever, but I guess I'll take it.

~

Years later, my friend at the barn, Meaghan, decided we were going to start intense lunge line lessons. She was the handler, lunging my horse Vador for me while I was astride, bareback and without reins. She had this vision of what I absolutely had to know, and she was going to teach me. I didn't understand her fervor but went along, happy to have a friend doing horse activities.

We warmed up with transitions. Upward transitions, going faster from walk-trot and trot-canter, were easy. But the downwards transitions, canter-trot, trot-walk, walk-halt, all without any reins or saddle, proved more difficult.

Meagan, who was older and much more experienced at showing than I, insisted that I do them to perfection. She made this her mission for some reason over the next two or three days. I still do not know and have never asked what possessed her to give me these lunge lessons, but they were, without a doubt, some of the most influential lessons I ever had. Once I realized I could do it, I used my seat so much more in my downward transitions, and made it a game of how little rein I could use in everyday riding.

But the truly unique aspect of these lunge lessons was Meagan's insistence that I be able to get off of a moving horse, while she was lunging it, at the walk, trot, and canter, and land on my feet. I instantly thought back to my forced fall training, and found it funny that this was still a forced fall, but now with "stick the landing."

"The trick is vault off how you normally would, but push yourself away more, look at the horse's head as you go down, and turn a little like you are going to move forward, parallel to them while they move away. When you land move your feet like you are running."

I didn't really have a choice in the matter and we started getting off at the walk, which was easy enough. Since Pepper's run away I had gotten off a few times while the horse was still walking, although I hadn't given it too much thought.

The trot was something new, but Meaghan said something familiar,

"Pick a shoulder and push off right as it pushes off the ground going forward, it will give you more momentum and make it easier."

Meaghan urged Vador into a trot and I sat it, holding the mane in front of the horse's shoulders to prepare for my vault.

One, two, one, two, one, two... I sat, feeling his trot rhythm, this time around I was much more aware of where my horse's feet were and was able to push off right after I felt his outside shoulder hit. I went sailing over Vador and smoothly careened over to the other side, where I promptly landed right on my backside.

"You didn't land on your toes. You have to land on your toes and run, not plant your foot down!"

I rolled my eyes and got up, brushing all the dirt off me, which was essentially all over my legs. Meaghan gave me a leg up and back at it we went again.

One, two, one, two... I leaned forward to the shoulders again and pushed with both hands, lifting my right leg up and over and then back down.

"TOES!!" Meagan screamed while I was in mid-air. She was in full trainer mode.

I did manage to point my toes, and bend my knees, I landed, awkwardly, running a little sideways before I could pick myself upright. Before I had enough time to collect myself my horse was stopped and Meagan was squatting down with her hands ready to toss me up.

"BETTER, NOW AGAIN!"

And we did do it again. And again. And again, until my landing was pretty good and glided along. I was really glad we were using Vador for this, he was smooth, easy to ride, but also very calm, and not bothered by much. Least of all a pair of teenagers doing this relentless circus practice. Meagan was thorough, and made me dismount at the trot from both sides until I was proficient. Nearly an hour, and half a dozen butt plants, passed by.

I thought we were done.

"Ok, Now the canter,"

I must have given her a *you have got to be kidding* look because she continued on with justification,

"Yeah, girl, canter! What are you going to do if this horse takes off and you can't stop it? Just hang on? No! You're gonna stop it, and if you can't stop it you goin' to get off right then and there...now!"

She had an interesting almost southern way of speaking, which I thought was odd because she was definitely born in Michigan. She did show horses a lot in Kentucky, so that might be where she got it from.

There was no point in arguing so I stood next to Vador, for what felt like my fiftieth leg up.

Meaghan smiled a little bit, pleased with her plan. Meaghan was a kind, almost naive soul, who always seemed to rub a few people the wrong way. I never understood that because she was so nice and helpful to everyone. Some people say you can be "too nice" but I never understood that. Kindness is in short supply, and someone doesn't have to have too much for another to have too little.

Like what she was doing now, spending the better part of an afternoon to help someone younger than her be a better rider. She didn't have to do that. No one asked her to. It was just in her nature to help. Despite my complaints, I knew that this was an awful nice thing Meghan was doing and I was thankful that she was doing it. Truthfully, I would be a little sad if she made me stop. Teenagers seem to be like that, actions not always matching feelings. We push away a bit to see if folks will hold onto us, to find out if they are genuine. Meaghan was, she meant it, whatever her reasons.

"Ok, tell him to canter and we will talk about it,"

I cued Vador from the walk going left, and he instantly responded and made his way into a nice, balanced canter.

"Ok, feel your lead?" Meaghan asked, hope in her voice.

"Yep!" I responded.

I could feel his left leg reaching out farther to the inside with my hands too, which were resting on the shoulders, his hard muscles holding me, holding the balance of the circle. To me, the canter feels like a heartbeat. It's comforting, calming, and I felt like I could just stay up here forever. Hurling myself off seemed almost a crime. But Megan's sweet southern-ish voice broke my spell,

"When you feel the lead touch down, and then that moment where all four feet are in the air, that is when you vault off. Same deal, land on toes, and run a bit."

I nodded my head and continued cantering along, counting the steps until I felt one that I liked.

Da, duh, one, da duh, two, da duh, three, I felt all the steps and decided on five. *Da, duh, four, da duh, five...* and off I went.

This is the closest to gymnastics I was ever going to get, and I felt like I was vaulting off a balance beam. As I leaned forward and pushed off his shoulders with my hands, I had a feeling that I should stick my chest out and up, making myself taller and sending my weight more upwards, off of the middle of me. I lengthened myself, stretching as I had seen ballerinas do, and pointed my toes. I landed with a little jog step to watch Vador canter along without me.

"That was great. Whoooooooooooo! Go girl! "She looked like a kid who'd been got told she was going to Disney World. She was so happy, full of joy, and cotton candy pink in the face.

I couldn't help myself but a huge smile spread over my face, and I put my head down a little bit in slight embarrassment. Meghan turned Vador into me and gave me a huge bear hug, running in place and bouncing around as she did.

"THAT WAS SO AWESOME!"

I just giggled, a little shocked that I just vaulted off a horse.

"Wait," Meghan regained her composure and got all serious trainer faced again. "You have to do it the other way too!"

I rolled my eyes and chuckled a bit.

"All right" I didn't really protest, I just needed to give the illusion I was going to.

Vador was standing there like a gentleman, lunge line on the ground, not moving a muscle. What a good boy.
To the right was a little more awkward, I did stick the landing but it wasn't as smooth. I made a mental note to get off on the right more anyway, so that it was more natural.
Meghan was beaming after our dismounts.

"Thank you for teaching me all that. I have never done anything like it." This was a huge confidence boost not just in riding abilities, but that someone, especially someone in more of a peer role, would take the time to teach me something, just because they thought I could do it. I was blessed to have this happen many times in my life, but I am always astounded by it, the selflessness, the kindness of it. It's the sort of life changing, radical kindness the world needs more of.

"You're welcome, you never know when you might need it" She replied. Eyes bright and happy at her accomplishment. I think she was just as happy that she taught me to do it, as I was at doing it.

And I did need it, literally a month later.

~Adult Reflections~

While scary, learning to fall is critical. You might get hurt as you learn to fall, but you will definitely get hurt if you don't. The fall practice is more for body awareness, so you know where you are in space, and potentially, you can protect a vulnerable piece of you, like your head. This should be practiced with supervision under the control of a qualified riding instructor.

My bareback lunge lessons with Meaghan are some of my most cherished childhood memories, and definitely in the top ten lessons I had ever had. The seat control I learned from the transitions has been a lifelong skill that I have continued to cultivate.

More immediately helpful was getting off a moving horse. This is a skill folks should have if they are going to show or trail ride — or ride anywhere outside of a controlled environment. There are MANY situations where you need to get off a moving horse, safely and quickly. Meghan knew I would be in these situations and choose to teach me until I got it perfect. In doing so, she saved my butt countless times, or at the very least made my life easier.

Many Runaway Horses

Off…Right Now!

Helen owned about ten horses, but the one she let us kids ride the most was Sampson.

Sampson was a Halflinger. Halflingers are built like a draft horse but a little sportier, compact, adult carrying workhorses. Rarely over fifteen hands (a "hand" measures 4") with tan-colored bodies and a bleached-blond, thick, wavy, mane and tail, they look like a *Barbie* horse. Sampson was primarily trained to be a cart horse, and every now and then Helen hooked him up and drove him around. We were allowed to ride him, but only at a walk and trot. Helen didn't want Sampson to canter and get to thinking that he could do that in harness too.

He was fat, fat, fat. He was so fat his back rose above his spine, creating a trough like valley down the length of it. The main reason Helen let everyone ride him was to try and keep his weight under control.

Because of how wide he was, Sampson was the default bareback horse. For some reason, bareback seemed to always be accompanied by riding in a halter and lead rope. I figured if we weren't going to tack up anyway, we could skip a step, tie a lead rope to the sides of the halter, and not have to go into the barn at all. Efficiency. Plus, Sampson steered pretty easily in the halter and was so lazy he wasn't in a hurry to go anywhere. It seemed pretty safe.

This is the same logic I brought with me when my friends, Maggie and Mikayla, went out riding past the rail road tracks into the back field. They tacked up like normal people, and I puttered along behind, far behind on Sampson, bareback, with a halter and lead rope reins.

"Let's run around the field" Mikayla prompted the group. The oldest of us, she often took up the leader role.

"Sure!" Maggie said with a sly grin, Her horse was faster than Mikayla's, and I am sure she wanted another opportunity to smoke her.

I, however, was not pleased with this proposition. Galloping bareback was not something I wanted to tackle. It isn't really the gallop that is hard to sit, it is the slowing down after the fact. I wasn't about to try it now, in the big open field for the first time. No, idiots do that. I also had a halter, not the best brakes if I need them. Not the right time to try and find that out either. Complete morons would do that. Most of all, Helen had specifically told us we were not allowed to gallop. I wasn't about to lose my ability to ride him by neglecting the rules.

"I can't!" I exclaimed as I gave them my best-*what are you thinking you morons? Of course I can't gallop on this horse-*face.

"What, you're afraid?" Mikayla taunted.

"To gallop on him? No," I gave her a quizzical look, wasn't this obvious?

"To gallop on him right now with no tack…yeah!" I motioned my hand to my lack of equipment. This was dumb and Mikayla was just being obtuse.

Maggie, to her credit, didn't say anything. While she didn't stand up for me, I could tell she thought Mikayla's idea was stupid.

"Plus," I continued, "Helen told us we can't canter or gallop him."

"Ok, you stay here then,"

Mikayla then gathered her reins and trotted off to a flatter spot to begin her run, Maggie rushed up to the side of her, eager to start at the same time so it could be a real race.

Ok Sampson, just eat some grass and they will be back. I didn't think anything of it, Sampson almost immediately dropped his head to devour the delicious, long, field grass. It was a nice day to just sit here and soak up the sun. I wasn't upset to be left behind, only that they didn't seem to get why. But no matter, I would just relax amongst the wildflowers and the nice breeze that carried its way over the field.

That plan failed.

The field was raised a bit off of the path we were walking, and the field's hills rolled quite a bit, obstructing the view of the whole plain, or anyone in it. As soon as the others were out of sight Sampson flung his head up from the grass, tensed his whole body to search for them, and took off at a full gallop to rejoin his "herd."

I was absolutely shocked, I didn't even think Sampson *could* canter, the big chunky monkey.

But he was cantering, no, GALLOPING after his friends. He was the left-out fat kid not picked for the soccer team and he was not having it. I sat back and pulled on those flimsy lead rope reins,

"Whoaaaaaaa!" I shouted in the deepest, calmest voice I could.

I might as well have been pulling on thin air. There was nothing at the end of that rope that was going to listen to me. By this point we had only run a few steps, I needed to do something fast-there was no way I was going to stay on like this. I had to get off, NOW. The left side (how one would normally get off) was where the manure was spread, and looked like it sloped up a little bit. This exit plan seemed likely to cause a trip and a roll under my obese runaway, so to the right it was. I flung myself off, staring at Sampson's head as I did, but instead of letting go, I decided I would try to stop Sampson and keep him from running off by leaning back a little into the rope to bring his nose around toward me.

It worked, but it made me fall back on my rear. Once I fell to the ground, still holding on to the lead rope, Sampson's head was jerked with my body weight hitting the ground. He whipped his head up in protest, rearing a bit, and leaning off the side away from me, ready to keep running.

Oh, no you don't! I scrambled to my feet and got a better grip on the rope, facing Sampson but backing into his hip to make him move his hips around so he couldn't run off.

Sampson responded to my request but let out an ear-splitting, belling shaking, whinny with a roaring snort to call for his friends.

We spun like this for a bit, Sampson flinging his head in the air and me backing into his hip and pulling it around to keep some kind of control. Eventually Sampson got sick of this and stood. Still high headed and thoroughly peeved, but not running off anymore. There was no way I was getting back on until they got back, but I went in search of a tree stump or a log or something close to the path, so they would see me when they got back.

Ugh.

This trail ride needed to be over like five minutes ago.

They emerged from the field a few minutes later and started to descend onto the path busting out laughing,

"We leave you alone for five minutes and you fall off?" Mikayla jeered.

"You can't ride the pony?" Maggie teased.

I was hurt, and a little shocked.

"Did you not just see what happened?" I asked, irritated.

"You mean you falling off, no, we didn't" Mikayla answered, she seemed to get some satisfaction out of being mean, Maggie not so much, but she followed the crowd at times.

"Uh...no," I answered, a little frantic to protect my reputation,

"Sampson took off after you guys left! He bolted after you. I got off."

"Sampson? Bolt? Yeah right! "

"Ok, Alex, tell yourself whatever you have to justify falling off."

"I didn't fall!" I said with a bit of a grunt as I abandoned the remounting stump idea, instead I belly flopped on Sampson, dug my foot into his flank, and weaseled my arm around his thick, top-heavy neck, wiggling on. Of course, he stood still as a statue, not typical of a horse that just took off.

We headed back, but to make matters worse Sampson poked around in the back, slow as ever. When we got back no one else believed what Sampson did either. Except Meaghan, the secret sage that no one seemed to know about,

"Yeah, I could see that, he doesn't get out much so he probably got a little herd bound."

She gets it!

"At least you did that emergency dismount I taught you!" She said with a wink and a twinkle in her eye.

~Adult Reflections~

I had ridden Sampson bareback, halter and lead around the farm and the arena countless times, and I always had good control.

But the nuance is: trail ride.

Things are different away from home, period. Horses act and react differently when out of the arena and in an open space.

Sampson also lived in a field with his buddies, and got taken out, still with his buddies, for rides. He didn't have any practice being apart from them or having them leave him. He wasn't trying to be "bad" per se, he was insecure at his solitary situation. Now, granted, his reaction was super dangerous, and needed to be stopped. I don't regret what I did at all, but that was the root of the problem.

How to avoid this?

As a general rule, don't go bareback with just a halter and lead rope on a trail ride. If you do, you better know that you will have total control in all situations.

Secondary to that, if you are going to do a lot of trail riding, the horse needs to be able to leave the group, and be left. This has to be practiced in more controlled ways (not people leaving to spontaneously gallop) and care needs to be taken to redirect the horse safely.

The infamous Sampson.

Spider-Horse

I absolutely lived at Wind Row. During the school year I would get there about 4:00 p.m. after school, and I would be there until way after dark. Every. Single. Day. I went every day in the summer, starting at about 8:30 a.m. and would be picked up around 7:00 p.m. Saturday, typically all day. The only day I didn't go with absolute certainty was Sunday.

I was there so much I got wrangled into all the chores, which of course, I didn't mind. Saturday mornings I would help clean the stalls with Helen and my friend Maggie. In the evenings I was often in charge of feeding the horses and sometimes even locking up the barn, as it closed at 9:00 p.m. I liked all the responsibility, and I took my jobs very seriously.

During the summer I even got paid to do all the morning chores plus stalls for thirty horses with one other worker. I went to lunch often with Helen, The Cowboy, and The Quiet One. The Cowboy Duo took me to lots of tack stores, horse pickups, feed store runs, and all sorts of random horse travel. I went along happily. I was in the truck with all of them just about as much as I was riding.

Many, many people thought that I was the child of Helen or The Cowboy Duo. Many times, they responded with, "Well, she is our adopted daughter" with a big smile on their faces, or, "She might as well be with how much we see her," with a bit of a chuckle.

I love my mom, and she gave me all the love and opportunities that she could, but in many ways, these were the people who ended up "raising me." They taught me a lot of life lessons: the "cowboy way," responsibility, responding to adversity, overcoming fear, how to act and conduct myself professionally. They taught me about the horse industry. I didn't realize it at the time, but they gave me all the structure and order to my life that I badly needed, but didn't know how to ask for. These folks did what my mom could not, mostly because of the circumstances at the time, but I needed what they had to give.

The farrier that came to Wind Row, Don, started to bring his son around one summer. I think his plan was to show him the ropes of being a farrier. I had observed that he had been letting the boy pull shoes off the horses and handing him some tools. The boy had the typical fourteen-year-old look: long and lanky, with a mop of brown hair that was neither short nor long, just a longer bowl cut that was constantly in his face and flipped up at the ends. He was cute.

Being so involved in the horse scene it seemed only natural that I should try to get with a "horse guy" and this seemed like a logical fit. I was told most of my life that guys should make the first move, so I strutted about with makeup on, leading my horse past the tack up stalls where they were working a little too often. I was trying to drum up interest in me.

To be honest, I can't even remember his name now. Let's call him Joel. Joel was definitely looking at me as I passed by, and I would goof around and talk to Don, hoping that Joel would butt in and talk to me. He did in fact not talk to me, he mostly looked at the ground. *Oh, he is just shy, he just needs a little push!*

"This here is my son, Joel," Don formally introduced him one day, and as he did Joel managed to pick his chin up from the floor and give me a quick darting look and small finger wave before staring back at the cement.

"And this is Helen's, the barn owner's, daughter Alex" he pointed to me, I didn't correct him, I might as well have been.

"Nice to meet you" I said in the sweetest voice I could muster and put my hand out for him to shake it.

He seemed a little taken aback by this and softened his somber look a bit and shook my hand, more eye contact now.

"Do you ride, Joel?" I asked him. Asking if he rode seemed to be an easy segue.

"Uh… no, I don't, I just help my dad." Rats. Okay, I needed to think quickly.

"Well, next time you come out, if you want, I can teach you the basics if you have time. We have plenty of horses to ride around here." Okay, all he had to do was take the invitation.

"Uh…yeah, sure. If that's ok with you Dad?" He looked over at Don—whether for permission or an excuse to say no, I wasn't sure. Don just smiled really big, and looked over at me instead of him,

"Of course!" he replied.

" Awesome, I'll see ya around."

Play it cool, Alex, don't be too excited or too desperate. I gave Joel a coy smile as I spun on my heel to walk away. He didn't know what hit him.

Don came by once a week, on Tuesdays, to do the horses. The following Tuesday I had a plan all worked out: I was going to have Joel just walk around a bit on Sampson. He was a "guy's horse" thick and burly. He didn't look girly-well, he did look a *little* girly with the blond mane and tail. At any rate Sampson had a manly name, was strong, and would be the perfect choice to get Joel hooked on riding. Plus, Sampson was slow, and pretty easy to ride most of the time. Sampson never did anything too naughty, save that bolting episode, but those were extenuating circumstances.

I was ready to go, but didn't want to seem too ready. Plus, I knew that Joel did still have some work to do with his dad. My plan was to wait about twenty minutes before noon, when Don would take a lunch break, then go and collect Joel for the riding lesson.

I purposely stayed away from where they were working and rode the horses I needed to ride that morning. I was a cool horse girl, I had stuff to do and I certainly wasn't waiting around for him.

With the last horse I was going to ride, I walked by where they were working. Don seemed more excited that I was coming to get Joel, than Joel was,

"HI ALEX!" he said with a booming voice.

"Hi Don, hi Joel" I answered back.

"Hi," Joel said back with that little wave again, a little more interest in the eyes.

"In about an hour or so, wanna do that ride?" I asked him. It was up to him, after all.

"Oh, yeah" he said, nodding his head a little too fast and nervous. Cute.

"Okay great, see ya in a bit," I said, and walked away without looking back.

I figured I would ride this horse, quickly put it back, then get Sampson by myself and lead him over to the tack up area. I wanted all my interactions with Joel to be perfect so I couldn't spare extra time where I wasn't totally on it.

When I finally brought Sampson over, Joel was pretty much leaning up against the tack up stall, waiting for me. That was cute. I didn't know how to start this conversation so just lead with, "Ya ready?"

I don't remember if he responded because I just would not shut up after that. I talked about how to brush and how to pick out their feet, as I was doing it. The foot thing was a little redundant, he had that part down working with his dad. Duh.

I tacked Samson up in some western tack and explained all the while I was doing it. I should have let Joel do some of it, but I just wanted him to see me as knowledgeable and smart, so, I did it. I got him a helmet, which looked ridiculous on that mop of a head, I doubted he would see anything with the helmet squishing the hair already in front of his eyes. He did a head toss to get the bangs to the side before the helmet went on, and while he looked dreamy doing it, the helmet made me question his hairstyle choice.

I realized I had been talking too much, and it was a decent walk up to the arena, so I figured I should ask him about himself. I stopped spewing horse information long enough to blurt out,

"So...uh... what do you like to do for fun?"

"Uh, well, I like dirt bikes," Typical. Every guy likes dirt bikes.

"Oh yeah? Do you race?" That seemed to be the thing to do if you rode dirt bikes.

"Yeah, actually my first one is in a few weeks."

"That's pretty cool, what do you have to do for the race?" I could care less about dirt bikes, but I did like competitions, and I could relate to that.

He yammered on about what was required of the race. I nodded a few times to show I was listening, but I was just waiting for him to stop. This was getting boring. But maybe I could get him interested in horses instead. By the time he shut up, we were in the arena, and I explained how to get on the horse,

"I'll hold him, you'll climb up on this block, put your left foot in the stirrup and swing your leg over, landing gently and being sure not to whack him in the butt with your foot."

Joel walked up the block pretty confidently, but then stopped and stared at the apparatus that was the saddle and drew a blank.

"Wait, what?" he seemed a little scared. Poor boy. I repeated myself, careful to be sweet about it,

"I'll hold him, you'll climb up on this block, put your left foot in the stirrup and swing your leg over, landing gently and being sure not to whack him in the butt with your foot."

"Yeah, I got that, but how do you not do that?"

"Not do what?"

"Hit him with your leg? He is so wide; I don't think I could get my leg over that far."

"Sure, you can…you just do it." I couldn't help myself but I shrugged my shoulders. Come on, man, this is obvious.

Joel did not seem to like this questioning of his ability and started to mount anyway. He put his foot in the stirrup, then he slowly and stiffly held onto the saddle, causing it to roll a little bit towards him. At this he picked up the pace, swinging his leg over too fast and slammed down on Sampson's back. Sampson wasn't bothered, but I was a little irritated that he didn't follow instructions. I said *gently*! I knew I needed to be nice so I corrected with,

"Ok, so we want to sit a little gentler on his back, it's kinder to him. And throw your weight over to the right, your saddle slipped and we need to straighten it."

Joel did listen this time, but he did it without hesitation in a jerky movement. While I couldn't put my finger on this, I didn't like how he did it. Slower would have been better, less jarring to the horse. Didn't he care?

At the risk of sounding nitpicky I let this one go, and showed him how to hold the reins,

"Four fingers on, thumbs on top, no pinkies," I held the reins first to show him, then handed them off to him, and he surprisingly picked them up correctly right away.

"If you want to go right, right rein, left leg. Left is left rein, right leg." This is what I remembered other instructors saying to beginners. I, of course, knew it was a little more nuanced than that, but this seemed a good place to start. I continued with the basics,

"Both legs squeeze until he goes, then no more squeezing. Pull back on both reins to stop. Once he stops you stop pulling."

Joel was sitting like he was playing video games in a chair with his feet up. His back was rounded like a bug and his feet pushed out like a skier, his toes in front of Sampson's shoulder. He did still hold those reins correctly in his hands, but had since lifted them high and straightened his arms out like he was going to balance a serving tray on them.

Ok, this teaching people thing is harder than I thought. There is just so much wrong.

I knew that I couldn't say *all* the things he was doing wrong or I would sound like I was picking on him, so I decided to let it go, Sampson didn't seem to mind and if they went anywhere, it would be at a snail's pace anyway. I would let Joel carry on and see if he could just walk around. That would probably work.

"Ok walk him forward."

Joel gave a little kick and Sampson crept forward. Immediately as he went to walk, Joel pulled back on the reins, moving his already high hands up to his armpits.
Sampson of course stopped, with a pained look on his face as Joel continued to pull. His mouth open and head up, twisting his big head to get away from all the pressure.

"Okay he stopped, no more pulling." It took a second but eventually Joel listened to my command, slowly lowering his arms back to their original too-high position.

"So, when he goes forward, don't pull, and even when you want to stop you don't need to pull that hard. It is actually really light pressure."

"But I did want him to stop, and he is so big!" he wanted to make sure I understood.

"Well, he is big, but that doesn't mean you have to pull on him," I said, maybe a little too defensively.

Sweet Alex, be nice.

"Let's try that again, only don't pull at all, just walk with him a bit, I'll walk right next to you."

He gave a little nod and urged Sampson forward. Sampson walked off, slower this time. Joel, to his credit, didn't pull back and we walked around like this for a few minutes. When it looked like Joel had relaxed a bit I directed,

"Okay, light little pull till he stops."

Joel raised his hands a bit and Sampson stopped easily. This time Joel gave the reins back to him as he halted.

"That really worked!" he had a bit of a glint in his eye. This was working.

"Now, turn him in a circle to the left." Joel did so, still awkward, but he got it done. He looked proud of himself. "Now to the right."

Joel turned Sampson easily in a little circle to the right, leaning a bit as he did, like he was on his dirt bike. I knew he shouldn't do this but I couldn't break it to him, especially since he seemed to be having a little fun. So instead, I said,

"Yeah! You got it!"

He rewarded me with a huge smile. This is great, before long we can be riding together, as a horse couple, how cute we could be!

"Now take him around this half of the arena and ride him along by the wall."

I spun and pointed out the route I wanted him to take. He could have some independence now, but not the whole arena in case I needed to get to him. Joel excitedly pushed Sampson into a walk and plow reined him around to the edge of the arena. It was rough but he was successful at getting Sampson to walk along next to the wall, or the rail as we call it. Joel started to get a little bit of swagger to him. He was feeling like a cowboy and was enjoying himself more. I don't blame him. There is so much confidence that comes from directing a huge animal and having it listen to you, bonus points if it is effortless. He was experiencing that confidence that I felt; it was awesome to watch. I figured he would thank me for it, which was bonus points in the potential girlfriend department.

He had almost made his half arena lap and was just about to pass the door where the horses came in and out. The door never closed all the way and there was a two foot or so gap between the door and the wall. People always stopped by the door and yelled "DOOR!" and waited for someone to respond before they entered.

As they were approaching the door, Sampson was inching closer and closer to it, eying the gap. I didn't want Joel to scrape his leg on the door or on the post after the gap so I called out to him,

"Left rein right leg, get off the wall a little bit. You are too close to that door."

Either he didn't hear me, or he didn't think he was close to the door. Or perhaps he thought I was acting like a mom, overbearing and over protective. Either way, he didn't touch the rein or even think about moving Sampson over. He looked straight ahead, riding along.

"Joel! Move him over!" I yelled, a little more insistent. He was going to scrape against it!

Sampson tipped his nose towards the outside to look at the gap. Joel was oblivious. *Sampson you can't fit through there, you goof!* I thought Sampson would probably stop and look out the door since Joel wasn't directing him otherwise. He wouldn't get out, being almost five feet wide (not really, but it seemed like it) he would only be able to stick his jug head through.

Joel continued to do nothing; this guy might not be boyfriend material.

Sampson stopped and curled his big, hefty neck surprisingly nimbly in between the gap and stuck his head out. Getting no resistance from poor Joel he then continued on, pushing his shoulder into the door, and started revving that powerful pulling horse engine of his. His shoulder slammed into the door with a loud BANG and the huge twenty-foot door swayed back and forth wildly. Sampson shimmied himself along with the door. Joel cried out and put both of his hands on the door and the post frame as Sampson kept rocking back and forth, trying to get free.

I was stunned. My mouth was probably open, too stunned to speak for a second. No way was this happening. And what could I do? I didn't know, but I started running over to them.

"Get off!" I don't know how he would but this seemed like a logical thing to say.

"I can't! I'm stuck!" Joel looked back again at me for help, panic in his eyes. This was bad. How could I help him? I ran right up to the side of Sampson and Joel to see if I could do anything, anything at all.

Sampson kept rocking the door with everything he had, determined to free himself from his directionless rider and arena prison. Joel had his arms spread out at maximum length pushing on the door and the frame, trying to lift himself clear upward off of the horse. There was no way he could actually get off, Sampson's girth scraping along the sheet metal that covers the door and the post. Joel's legs were pinned between the door and the horse, he was just as stuck as Sampson. We also hadn't gotten to the point in the lesson where we covered dismounting. So, he was doubly stuck.

Mind racing, and seeing how pinned they were, the only think I could do was run out of the arena. There was another exit that had a board across it that I could duck under, and go around to the front and try to push Sampson backwards. Yes, that is what should happen. I could do that.

"I have to go around and push him back out." I told Joel.

"Push him? What!" Joel clearly didn't get it, and there was no time to explain.

But as I went to spin on my heel and attempt to run around the building Sampson did a bit of a jump up, all four feet off the ground. *He can jump?* This horse can barely lift his leg for the farrier, let alone jump!

Joel went up with Sampson, still holding onto the sides, sliding his hands along as he went up. The jump must have been the thing that dislodged Sampson from the vice grip he was in because he shot out of the door as he landed, galloping frantically down the breezeway and into the driveway. Joel's hands were still on the door and the post, but now, being free of Sampson, his legs also splayed out to hold himself upward, one foot on the door and the other on the post. He was twisted around trying to hold himself up and clearly in shock that he didn't fall off, but was instead a spider up on the wall watching Sampson race off without him.

His shock didn't last long as he let go and descended to the ground. I ran up to him, but after briefly pausing to giving him a quick once over, I ran past him, threw my head back and yelled, "You, okay?" He was standing, and miraculously his jeans hadn't been ripped up.

He nodded, I think, and watched me race after Sampson.

I mean, Joel was fine, at the very least he was standing and not bleeding, but Sampson could run into the road or get hung up on something. The obvious choice was to rescue Sampson. Joel could stay there; he was no help anyways and didn't listen to directions.

I chased after Sampson for twenty minutes. He raced over to the mare's pastures and squealed at them over the fence. They turned to kick him but thought better of it because of the electric wire. When I got close to him, yelling at him to get away from the mares, he did exactly as I asked and ran to the back pasture where his friends were. Sunny, Flash, Gator, and Freckles. When I got over there, sweaty and out of breath, he ran away again, this time back to the barn by his stall. By the time I jogged my way over there, exhausted from running over the whole farm, Sampson was munching on grass and let me grab him no problem. Of course.

    Since Helen's tack room was by her stalls, I was able to untack Sampson over there and just grab a halter and lead him back to his far pasture, out of sight from everything else with the gelding gang. I turned Sampson out but stayed out in the pasture for at least an hour, hiding under some trees and feeding Flash grass that I pulled out of the ground and then handed it to him. I was not going to the barn until Joel and his dad left. I was mortified. My plan to impress Joel had completely gone up in flames.

    He would never ever talk to me again, and I didn't want him to. This was the most embarrassing thing of my entire life. Can't even teach someone to walk around on the Haflinger! But also… the Haflinger!

    Sampson, why on Earth did you do that! He had never done that before! I wallowed in self-pity and woe- is- me- the- world- is- out- to- get- me-sorrow until I was sure an hour had passed. I crept back, hugging the pastures to look for Don's truck. If I saw it, I would dart back in with the horses. But as I stuck my neck out around the barn his truck was gone. Whew!

    Everyone, including Helen, had heard all about my little mishap and ribbed me for it constantly. Surprisingly, no one was mad, or very surprised. Their main take away was not what Sampson did, but that my little love bird stunt had gone array.

    Joel did not come the next week and Don didn't mention anything. Joel did come a few more times, but I avoided him completely and we never talked again. Which was probably for the best because what would I say?

    Sorry you spider-climbed the wall instead of riding the horse?

Sorry I was too embarrassed to come and check on you after I caught Sampson?

Sorry I put you in this position in the first place?

Sorry you hate horses now and we have nothing in common?

There wasn't anything to say, although I should have checked in on him.

-Adult Reflections-

To think this was technically the first riding lesson I taught! I don't get embarrassed too often-life is after all essentially a comedy-but this one was bad. I felt awful about it and I did so much wrong. For starters, always be in a 100% secure area with beginners. NO GAP. CHA instructor certification covers this in depth.

People will almost never have the correct position to start with, give them what to do, not what not to do. Set parameters. You might need to physically move an arm to where it is supposed to go so they can get the feeling of it. I severely underestimated how to teach someone, and how to set realistic goals.

All elements of a beginner lesson should be set up for success. I firmly believe in starting people off on the lunge line; students can learn proper position without worrying about control. Obviously, this was not on my radar at the time.

I obviously under estimated Sampson. Sampson was quiet and lazy, but truthfully, not very broke. That is why he did crazy things randomly and seemingly out of nowhere.

Finally, while I admire my go-getter spirit, it is definitely better not to convince someone to like you, or concoct this elaborate scheme to get them to be your boyfriend. Just be, people will come along.

The horse world is a terribly small place. Years later I ended up marrying a farrier. My husband, when he was just starting out as a farrier rode around with Don a bit, and Don ended up giving him quite a few clients.

Guess I have a thing for farriers.

That Time I Almost Got Hit by a Car

It wasn't until much later in life that I truly understood what trespassing was; mostly because adults frequently went into large, open, vacant, spaces and I passively followed along. They would usually say, "We aren't supposed to be here... but..." and continued on forward.
This was certainly the case with what we referred to as "the power lines," given that it was owned by the power company and housed huge metal towers for the high voltage electric lines.

To our credit I don't think there was a sign that warned us to *KEEP OUT*. There certainly wasn't a fence or a gate, in fact, there was a path leading right from the road and down alongside the power lines. We were easy opportunity trespassers, but we did it none the less.

It all started when a group of us wanted to go trail riding, which really meant road riding. Adults and kids set off one Saturday afternoon down the road towards the field with the power lines, packed for a good three-hour journey with water and saddlebags. The field stretched for quite a while, and you could hear the faint buzz of the electric lines above. Those towers look so cold and menacing, almost like something out of a science fiction novel. I knew that you could touch the poles and not get shocked, but I still wasn't going to take any chances and stayed far away.

Time is not reliable in childhood, but I think it took about forty minutes or so to ride the length of the powerlines to another open field that might have been private property. One reason it took so long was this was a walk-only trail ride. Horses cover about three and a half to four miles an hour at a walk, so by that logic the whole stretch was probably just under three miles. But who knows? It could have been less than a mile and I was just bored. The whole time I was scouting out the galloping possibilities of this stretch, it was flat, not too soft, nor to hard, there was plenty of room to pull up, and it was wide enough for multiple horses. It was even pretty, with white wild flowers fluffing up the sides of the path. It was the perfect galloping spot.

My friends and I formed a plan: we'd go to the powerlines again, just us, to gallop it. I decided I would ride Sampson, since at this point Helen had somewhat removed the cantering restriction. Well, he could gallop, trot, and walk, but not canter. Helen figured he would be able to discern the difference. She approved of the power line idea and the use of Sampson, so our plan was a go.

A few days later we were off. It took a good thirty minutes to get to the power lines from the barn, down a few dirt roads to reach the great wide-open field. Sampson, as always, was lagging in the back. I had put his previous transgressions behind him, but I was armed with a western saddle, bit and bridle for our run debut. I knew this track was super long and Sampson wouldn't be very fast and would get tired quickly, but I thought it would be fun to run along on his stubby, short, little legs.

Trail rides are either silent or filled with chatter,it is an easy way to catch up with your friends. Since my mount was slow, I was definitely removed from the conversation a bit, and my friends would have to stop every now and then to wait for me to catch up. I could hear wisps of their conversation about the latest boy they were interested in and who was making use of the latest technological advancement: texting. Cell phones were really catching on; now that I had cell phone I could text, too, but I only had so many minutes that I could use. Texting used up one minute for every three texts. It was really hard to text someone then. There was no keyboard per se: you used this system called T9, where every number on your phone had three different corresponding letters. 2 was ABC, 3: DEF, 4: GHI, 5: JKL, 6: MNO,7: PQRS,8: TUV, and 9: WXYZ. If you wanted a particular letter, you had to press the number as many times as it took to get to that letter, and when you saw it appear on the screen you had to stop, or go and do it over again. So, for example if you wanted to say: "I am busy," it would be:

4 three times
0 for a space
2, 6
0
2 twice
8 twice
7 four times
9 three times

    It was really a frustrating business and incredibly time consuming. I didn't understand how people could just sit there and text each other, it took forever. Just call!

    Come to think of it, I didn't bring my phone with me, I left it in my tack locker. Those two were attached to their phones so I bet they brought theirs.

    "Did you guys bring your phones?" I asked them.

    "Uh...you know, I don't think I did," Maggie answered, looking at Mikayla to see if she had brought one,

    "No, I left it at the barn,"

    Wow, they really weren't attached to their phones.

    "Me, too," I continued "I just wanted to take a picture of the wildflowers in the field."

"They are really pretty, I have flowers like that by my house," Maggie said. I am not sure if that was a one-up move, or an attempt to relate. You could never tell with her.

I missed my phone even more when we got to the field. The left side was lined with Queen Anne's lace plants that were at least two feet tall. They swayed a little with the gentle breeze of the day, and their brilliant white contrasted with the green field bathed in sunlight. I know the plants are often considered a weed and invasive, but I liked how they looked all cloaked together like that, a blanket of white.

We had decided that we should trot a bit in the field to get the horses warmed up, and so they didn't get to thinking that they got to run every time there was an open space. We turned the front of the field into our own personal arena, trotting around and making circles. Well, they cantered, I just trotted because Sampson wasn't really balanced enough to canter circles, but he would be fine in the straight line of the run lane.

Mikayla set the pace and she pulled up her big grey warmblood gelding, named Onyx, to a halt and waited for the rest of us to do so when she was done warming up.

"Ready?" she asked, a little devilish, she knew what was coming. Galloping, especially in an open space like that is its own kind of drug.

"Oh yeah!" I yelled. Sure, I wasn't going to go fast, but I was excited all the same.

"You bet!" replied Maggie.

She was on another one of Helen's horses, Sunny, who was an older Morgan. Maggie had ridden Sunny around a bit but I don't think she'd ever galloped him. Hershey, her own horse, was a poor choice for field galloping because she was difficult to stop.

We all got in line, single file, Mikayla in front and me in the back. Mikayla urged Onyx into a canter, those big legs stepping high, full of natural impulsion and spring, and began to extend, flattening out, into the gallop. It was cool to watch Onyx go from this naturally collected canter, to pulling his nose outward and downward, lowering his neck and flattening the curve in it. Mikayla went with him just the right amount. Hands forward, eyes up, raised out of the seat but still in the middle of it. Her leg was textbook perfect, heel down, heel under hip, and calves rock solid and steady, never swaying, ever. She kept this position as Onyx eased his way into the gallop. I couldn't help but to think how elegant it was. I was even a little jealous.

Sunny was looking to go, but Maggie sat deep and held him back to let Onyx get ahead. Sunny had a quick, slightly choppy gait, and he provided a sharp contrast to Onyx. When there were about ten horse lengths between them, Maggie let Sunny go, and he charged forward, really pushing hard with his hind legs and sprung right into the run to catch up. His arched neck quickly moving back and forth, gaining speed. He reminded me of a cat leaping after a mouse.

If we were to compare to birds, Onyx would have been eagle, big and majestic, Sonny would have been a hawk, quick and explosive but still with style, and Sampson, well, Sampson I think would be more like a penguin. Yes, a penguin; plodding along, unable to fly.

Sampson did not slowly gain speed; he did not spring forth and shoot out from under me. No, he cantered at first at the prospect of being left behind by his friends, but no amount of urging could get us closer to the others. Onyx was long gone, maybe fifty horse lengths away. Sunny was closer, perhaps twenty lengths away, but I still could not catch up to them. I kissed and gave him a little nudge with my heels every stride but it was no use. He was going this pace, barely over a canter, and no faster. There was nothing left in the tank. We carried on this way for quite some time, chugging along.

After a while, Sunny looked like he was struggling a bit ahead of me, and slowed a little with each step. He had really cranked it when they first took off, but now the distance was getting to him. Normally, you can't hear much in the thunder of hooves as you gallop, but today I wasn't thundering. I could hear Sunny's labored breathing over the lack of impact Sampson was producing.

In the distance, Mikayla had already pulled Onyx up and was waiting for us to come and meet her. Sunny still got there first, but Maggie had significantly slowed him down to save his lungs and Sampson, while still five or so strides back, chugged along at the same, slow pace until he plodded to a halt and almost instantly began eating grass. He was still breathing pretty hard but refused to give up on the munching. Classic. The other horses had a bit more sense and stood still, sides still heaving up and down, until they caught their breath enough to eat. Onyx came back to normal pretty quickly, and Sunny took a little longer but his heart did eventually come down to baseline, and he started nibbling a bit. Sampson took the longest since he was not only the least fit of the group, but had never actually caught his breath and had begun gobbling as if he was starving.

"Sunny is pretty quick for an old guy," I said to Maggie, turning my attention from Sampson's gluttony.

Sunny looked pretty good for being in his twenties. He was a classic bay, maybe 14.2 hands, and had a pizazz when he moved, flexing his joints and picking up his feet higher than other horses. It was a snappy movement that looked like it took a lot of energy. While Onyx had changed his energy flow to gallop, Sunny kept that same snap to him. He was old but he was proud, and he wasn't letting up.

"Yeah, that thrust at the beginning really got me, it was super forceful, I wasn't sure I was gonna sit it!"

We all laughed about the prospect of falling off when a horse starts to gallop and how embarrassing that would be. I for one, would be mortified. It was funny to think about because that wasn't going to happen to any one of us, not really.

The field continued on well on past our line of sight, but was too twisty to do a full out run. It then connected to a patch of woods and pasture, presumably private land, and we could follow that to an adjacent road, and make a loop back to the barn. That is what we did with all of the adults the other day, and we knew that would take close to two hours.

"I don't really want to go back all the way around in that loop" Maggie chimed in, motioning to the path.

"Yeah, me neither," Mikayla agreed.

"We could race back?" I offered.

My friends raised their eyebrows in agreement, and with big smiles, urged their horses into a canter. I had a leg up on them though, I turned a little before them, and was already off.

Now, I knew it was wrong to run a horse home. Every horse book ever says that it is wrong. I had even experienced the extreme barn storming with Pepper, running back that first day I owned her. But, in my mind, this was different. This was an informed decision. Sunny and Onyx were both well broke horses, and they were a little tired from this almost mile-long sprint. Sampson was a totally safe bet to run home on, given that he couldn't be bothered to run.
Or so I thought.

Sampson turned into a completely different horse. No longer the chubby Haflinger plodding along behind the others, he was now a ball of pure muscle using every ounce of his massive pushing and pulling power to lurch himself forward. Dirt was flying everywhere as he ate the earth up from underneath him, spewing it in every direction. I got that familiar whoosh of air forcing itself into my ears, blocking out everything else, and my eyes teared up as the wind blasted into them. I looked over my shoulder, and this time it was Maggie and Sunny close to me, and Mikayla was way behind.

It didn't even look like she was running. Maggie was, but she was no match for my pocket rocket pony, on a mission to win! I was slightly impressed with Sampson's competitive spirit. Maybe if I'd started towards the front in the first place he would have actually raced before. Or, it could just be that we were headed home and he just wanted to get back to his field and chow down on grass again.

It was great fun to be in the lead. *I am on the fastest horse... they can't catch me.* I liked this feeling and wanted it to last. Sampson seemed pretty full of himself too, not letting up, not even acting like he was tired. He must have been saving all this energy for an occasion such as this.

My lead secure, the road in view, and a good story to tell of the little fat pony that could, I figured I had better start pulling Sampson up. An exceptional stopping time from a dead run to a walk would be fifty feet, and that would be on a horse that has superb brakes. One hundred feet was more likely, but I was probably five hundred feet from the road at this point. I was well in the clear.

I relaxed my mind and muscles, and took my leg off, no longer urging Sampson to go faster. Often at this point, the horses will kill the engine and start to slow down automatically, as they are not being encouraged anymore. Sampson didn't slow at all, and charged on as he was when I was kicking him along.

Gee, he really likes this, okay buddy back off now. I sat back in the saddle and pushed my feet slightly forward, trying to counteract his forward motion with a little bit of backward motion, and put some light pressure back on the reins to ask him to come back to me. Horses don't often slam on the brakes at a run like this, they slow down maybe ten percent, a few moments later, another ten, and so on and so forth. It is not always even. It could be ten, thirty, sixty. Point being, you feel some deceleration, and then you go from there.
But Sampson didn't do anything.

No matter, I'll just need to get his attention. I started giving half halts on the rein, a check and release, pulsating rein cue in time with the stride. This doesn't give the horse something to pull against, and can do a lot to help a horse with lots of forward drive. I managed to get three or so in each of his gallop steps.

Hey! Hey! Hey! Pay attention!
Hey! Hey! Hey! Sampson!
Hey! Hey! Hey! SAMPSON!!!

By this point I was pulling his face off, half halting in a yank and jab motion that I would otherwise never do, but Sampson absolutely WOULD NOT STOP AND HAD NO INTENTION OF STOPPING. He was completely ignoring me, as if I wasn't there. He didn't even seem the least bit bothered by the punches to the face he was getting with the reins every stride. He didn't even toss his head in protest. It was as if they weren't happening at all.

By this point, the road was getting closer and I was getting worried. Sampson wasn't racing his friends; he was racing for home. He wanted to get back to the barn and was going to run, run, run, all the way there. It's about a mile of road riding back to the stable with some pretty awkward turns and often times a fair number of cars.

We needed to stop. NOW.

But how? Nothing had worked and we were going a little too fast for a one rein stop. Those really only work if you are not up to full speed yet, or you catch it in the first few moments of a bolt, like I did before with Sampson in the field. Attempting it at this speed, if it worked, could cause Sampson to trip, lose his footing, and fall down, possibly roll over. But not doing it would mean running down the road. I could just imagine Sampson side swiping a car and ramming my leg into the metal, shattering it to pieces.

I could equally see Sampson flipping over and crushing me completely with his massive weight as his colossal body met mine.

In that moment I decided it was more likely that something happens on the road. There were too many variables I couldn't control out on the road, but this was just me and him. It was worth the risk.

I leaned forward and slid my right hand down to the middle of his big massive neck, avoiding getting my hand tangled in his mop of thick, stringy mane. I closed my finger around the rein, tight so it wouldn't slip and threw my weight backward and yanked my hand up towards my hip. I expected him to yield his head and proceed to go into a tight circle until he stopped. Or that he would at least give his head a little, and then I could jab it over from there.

But instead, he tilted his head away from my rein pressure and pulled his head down, diving into the pressure and pulling against me. He meant business.
Immediately, I went to the other side and attempted the same thing but to the left, hoping for a better result.

Again, he rolled into the pressure and down, taking all the leverage I had away and pushing his full weight into my hand. It would be impossible to stop him.
I had run out of options. I had nothing else left to try, and the road was coming closer, maybe 300 feet away now. A feeling of true terror came over me. I was going on the road. I can't stop this horse.

Please Dear Lord Jesus just let this horse stop!

"WHAT ARE YOU DOING?" Maggie yelled out from behind me. Good, she knew something was wrong.

"I CAN'T STOP!" I yelled back. That seemed the appropriate response, it was accurate.

"WHAT DO YOU MEAN YOU CAN'T STOP?" her voice was angry, as if I was playing a game with her that she couldn't figure out.

"CAN'T STOP" I yelled back again, trying to be as clear and direct in a *of-course-I-am-not-joking-around-what-do-you-think-I-want-to-run-in-the-road-and-get-hit-by-a-car* kind of way, hoping she would understand.
And thank God, she did.

I have retold this story hundreds of times and I still can't believe what happened next.
Whether she saw it in a movie, read it in a book, or had some supernatural intuition as to what she should do, Maggie kicked Sunny up closer to us.

She is gonna try and cut us off. Brilliant!

I still made some half-hearted attempts to slow Sampson down. I knew they were in vain but I wanted to give Maggie some firsthand knowledge as to what was happening. No matter what I did, pull back, check back, reins side to side, one reins stop, absolutely nothing was stopping this horse. He was a true runaway train. He must have looked magnificent, with his golden body rippling from the effort of flying over the earth as he did, nostrils wide, blond mane and tail streaming back behind him with the wind.

He must have been the most beautiful thing to behold in the moment. Beautiful and terrifying. Unhinged and hell bent on getting home.

As Maggie got closer to us, I saw her face change into a determined scowl with just a little bit of fear behind her eyes. She saw that I was helpless. I was a lot of things, but never that. She urged that old Morgan faster and faster, closer to me. Soon Sunny's nose was at Sampson's hip, and then by my leg, and finally they were running in tandem, nose to nose, our legs bumping into each other every other step. The two geldings raced along in lockstep toward the road and time was running out.

There was no way she could get ahead of me to block Sampson's path, there wasn't enough time. The road was just under 200 feet now and getting closer every second. But there was a hint of hope. Maggie seemed to be sure of herself and her movements, like she knew what do, as easy as getting on a horse itself. Tying her fate to mine, she reached over the gap between the two horses and grabbed Sampson's rein with one hand. She latched on, holding onto Sampson tight, and pulled back on Sunny,

"WHOA, BUD...WHOA!"

Sampson, now next to another horse, and one that was also his pasture mate to boot, gave no protest and came back immediately. Maggie was able to steady herself and stay centered while guiding the two horses to a stop; half off of one of them. The sun shone on her, bathing her in glorious light as I lifted my head in bewilderment at what just happened. She had stopped the unstoppable horse. We had stopped in time, with about fifty feet in the field to spare before the road.

An engine roared ahead of us and a purple Trans Am, going about sixty miles an hour down the narrow dirt road, blazed by in a flash, sending the dirt and gravel crashing all around. I almost got hit by a car.

I almost got hit by a car!

"Dude, you almost died" Maggie said, almost matter-of-factly, in shock.

Mikayla cantered up easily and unbothered alongside us and asked Onyx to halt.

"What happened?" She didn't seem that concerned.

"Alex almost died is what just happened" Maggie snapped back, still in shock.

Mikayla looked at us puzzled and very confused.

"Yeah... uh," I started, still a little shaky and in disbelief of both my near-death experience, and how magnificently it had been avoided.

Mikayla looked a little annoyed, like she didn't understand. How could she not? Didn't she see what just happened?

"Sampson wouldn't stop. Like, WOULD NOT STOP. Maggie rode alongside me, grabbed my rein, and was able to stop him. Then, as soon as we did, that car passed us."

I breathed a shaky breath and looked down. This was serious business. I had almost thrown myself over the edge. It was so, so, so, stupid. I was embarrassed that it even happened. I should have never run back home. Every person ever says not to for this very reason. I thought it would be fine, but it clearly wasn't and I almost paid the ultimate price for my stupidly.

Maggie too was silent beside me, spooked by the whole thing, eyes wide and contemplating what had just happened.

"Well, I guess this is why they say to never run your horse in the homeward direction." Mikayla said, breaking the silence with a "duh" look on her face. She didn't run her horse back in the first place, because she knew the rule and didn't push it like we did. Still, she had to say it.

I looked at Maggie and lowered my voice to be as serious as possible,

"Thank you for saving me."

Maggie snuck out a brief smile, she was happy to be thanked, but I could tell it didn't occur to her that I would.

"Yeah, of course, you would have done the same thing."

I nodded and we rode off down the road together, at a walk this time, leaving Mikayla to bring up the rear. She didn't understand. She wasn't a part of this.

We, of course, anyone and everyone about our near-death experience. I was always sure to tell them that it was my fault, and it was Maggie who saved my life.

-*Adult Reflections*-

I knew I was wrong this time as soon as I did it. I knew not to run a horse home, but I thought it would be fine because Sampson was lazy, I had a lot of galloping experience, and that I was a decent rider and I could handle it. But these rules are there for a reason, and this was the last time I made a mistake like that. This experience, and how close it came to being deadly, taught me that the rules apply to *everyone*, and to stop using "yeah ...but..." excuses.

The main thing I can add now from training horses is that a horse has no business galloping if it is not, at minimum, solid at the canter in terms of pace control, steering, slowing down, and stopping. Short gallops should be attempted in an arena before going out into an open space like that. Even though Sampson was running home towards his friends, the real reason I couldn't stop him was his lack of training. I didn't know this nuance at the time, but of all the stories, this is the one I think of, and have retold the most.

I am so incredibly thankful to Maggie and what she did for me that day. How she reacted that fast and knew what to do is a mystery, even to her. The Lord answered my prayer, he did stop the horse, through Maggie. If it hadn't worked, Maggie could have been ripped off her horse at the gallop, descending down into the small gap between the two horses at high speed, hitting the hard ground and possibly getting clobbered by galloping hooves overhead. She could have been just as badly hurt as me if I continued toward the road. I don't think she thought about that though, she just acted, like a true friend.

Something like this bonds you to a person in a way that is a secret thread between the two of you, always tied together no matter how far apart. I still feel the thread, pulling at me just as she selflessly pulled Sampson up, all those years ago.

Is it Broke?

We used to play this game at the barn: *Is it broke?*

Is it Broke? -A game to test your bravery, stupidity, or both!
Instructions for play: any time a new horse comes to the barn with questionable experiences, from an auction, abandoned by someone, or with no information whatsoever, and/or the owner of the horse is just desperate for help, offer to get on the horse with no questions asked.
A key factor of the game is to not do any groundwork or attempt to understand the horse's level of training whatsoever. Just put the tack on and get on. Don't bother to do it in a small, confined area with few distractions either, just get on in the big indoor arena with all the people.
It is also crucial that there be a peanut gallery present with some sort of recording device, or at least their word, to recount the events should they go sideways.
Bonus points if you are too big to be riding the horse.
Now you are ready to play!

    We did this all the time, usually at the urging of the adults running the show. I can't really blame them, it was one less buck that they had to sit. We became a lot better at riding bucks, leaps, and antics ourselves. The horses however, could have done with better treatment and have been less scared in the first place if we had taken our time, but it didn't happen that way.

    There was a woman who paid board on a horse for one month and then promptly abandoned it, no more payment and no more contact with Helen. She had to go to court to get what was then called a stockman's lien, to take over ownership of the horse. She was, of course, going to sell the animal to try and recoup her lost board costs. She had no information on the horse, a full-bodied sorrel gaited mare we shall call Pippin, and the owner was AWOL. Maggie volunteered to hop on, one of the first instances of playing *Is It Broke?* Everything worked out just fine, Pippin was broke, and they were eventually able to sell her.

Sometimes a boarder would take on a rescue case from an auction, and would have no idea about the horse or what its training level was. Every now and then one would buck at the canter, but all of them seemed to be, at least at one point, riding horses. They had all at least been started under saddle. This unfortunately carried over to the miniature horses that were given to Helen, Toby and Stormy. Minis are not meant to be ridden at all. They are more designed for pulling carts, and can pull a lot relative to their size. A mini could pull two grown people in a cart fairly easily. But really only small children should ride minis, which is hard to do because the child also has to break the mini. We knew all of this, and I think that is why it was funnier, we weren't supposed to do it. The minis didn't seem to be in immediate pain, they didn't buckle under our weight as we got on them, and seemed to move normally. There was no struggling to move or heavy breathing, so I guess we figured we were in the clear.

Maggie would even trot around on Stormy, her legs dragging in the dirt as she did, laughing the whole time. Stormy and Toby were very attached to each other, so whenever Maggie brought Stormy out to goof off on, someone would bring Toby along so he wouldn't be upset and love on him. He had such a thick, shaggy forelock that I truly don't remember what his face looked like. It was fun to ruffle that big mop of a forelock around and Toby seemed to like the attention.

"Has anyone ever ridden Toby?" I asked Maggie one day, a little bored and in the mood for a little mini riding myself.

"Not that I know of. I've never seen it." Maggie replied while pulling Stormy back down to a halt. Stormy was cute, and was a whirl of grey, black striped hooves and molting around his eyes and muzzle. He looked like a little mini appaloosa.

I looked over Toby, plump and truly a brown horse. He looked uninterested in our proposition, but I also couldn't see his face on account of all the mane, so he could have been game.

My helmet was sitting on the observation room railing right next to me, and I could fashion reins out of the lead rope by tying them to the sides of Toby's halter, as Maggie had done with Stormy.

"You gonna try?" Maggie said with a sly smile. I knew she wasn't going to do it, but she wanted the spectacle of me giving it a go.

"I think so..." I said slowly. I was going through worse case scenarios in my head. Toby was, after all, a mini, and even if he took off and pitched me, how hurt could I really get?

At this point I had stopped counting all the falls I had had, but at last count it was at least twenty. In all that time I had never had a serious fall. Probability wise, this seemed like a safe bet. A little stupid, but safe. It would be fun.

I started fashioning the reins, clipping the lead rope to the left side, and tying the end of it in a knot on the right side of the halter. The rope reins were too big, looping down almost to his petite shoulder.

To my credit I did turn him in a circle off of each of my rope reins, and I walked him forward and stopped by pulling both of them back. He complied pretty easily and I figured that was all the prep work that could be done in this situation. Now to get on and cowgirl up!

Getting on a mini is a hilarious venture. Normally when you get on bareback, you swing your leg over from a

mounting block and grip it a bit onto the other side of the horse, then you push on the mane and try to shimmy yourself over to the middle of the horse's back. It takes a fair amount work and body awareness so you don't slip back off. With a mini, you stand on one leg, awkwardly swing your leg two and a half feet in the air until you are standing over top of them, straddling the mini.
It brings a laugh out of your chest just attempting it, it is so ridiculous.

Once I was over Toby, I stood over him with no weight on his back for a minute and gave him some aggressive neck rubs. It was likely he hadn't had a person over him in this way before, so I didn't want to scare him.
He didn't move, and didn't turn back to look at me as if to say, "Hey, what's going on?" No, he just stood, facing straight ahead as if I wasn't towering over him, seemingly indifferent.

Gaining confidence from this perceived lack of interest on his part, I slowly bent my knees and lowered myself down on to Toby's back, staggering my weight so he wouldn't experience it all at once. If he freaked out, I could just stand up. After a minute of silent, careful weight distribution I was on Toby's back. He remained uninterested and seemed calm, so after some more neck rubs that swayed his chunky neck back and forth, I gathered the reins and asked him to walk forward. Being as he didn't know how to walk forward off my legs, I made a "cluck, cluck" sound with my tongue between my teeth and a little tap on his rump and he swayed his way forward.

As soon as he took a step, I wobbled a bit side to side. There is no grip on that small back, just an area about the size of a dinner plate to sit, legs dangling and swaying around with virtually no way to settle them, and nothing to grip. I should have walked a bit longer to settle him in, but I was anxious to trot, and apprehensive that he might buck when I did. I wanted to get it over with, so I started squeezing my legs and clucking like before, seeing if he would pick up a trot. He was very uninterested about the whole thing, but after a few encouraging taps on the rump he eventually acquiesced to my request, and trotted forward.

A mini trotting is like popping popcorn, a violent popping around back and forth, quick, and with no real rhythm. It is so hard to stay up in the center of them! The leg swaying intensifies from the lack of gripping ability and my legs looked almost like I was jogging myself with how much they were moving.

But it was hilarious, I felt like a little kid getting jostled around on Grandpa's knee and thrown into the air occasionally. It was pure fun.

Toby, however, did not agree that it was pure fun and only trotted a dozen steps before he took off in a full-blown pony gallop. He threw his neck down to the ground and took off like a rocket.

Well, I've done it now...

I held on, barely, and tried to steer a little bit. I tried pulling the reins for getting his head up but it was no use. Toby's bolting soon turned to bucking as he ran as fast as he could and bucked every two strides or so in a wild fury. He even made this growling, almost roaring sound which I had never heard from a horse before, much less a mini. It was terrifying, was he going to attack me when I eventually fell off? I didn't think so, as horses are not typically aggressors, but I had also never ridden a mini, nor heard that roar before; so today was a new day.

As I started to slip off, I kept a close eye on Toby's head lest he swings around and tries to stomp me; I at least wanted to see it coming. But Toby's body was straight as mine left his and I relaxed a bit, I would go, alone, to the ground.

I had no expectations of a bad fall and didn't tense at all as I hit the ground.

It felt like there was a bomb inside my hip, exploding, searing with pain as the mushroom cloud of nerves firing sent the pain shooting up into my back and spread down my leg into my toes. This was the worst pain I had ever experienced, I had landed directly on my hip, slamming that bone into the ground.

The pain was paralyzing, my mind went into a fog of it and I stared straight ahead at the little gap in the wall to get from the arena into the observation room, unblinking, and unwaveringly focused. It didn't really make the pain go away, but just focusing on the feeling itself would be unbearable. Maggie slowly made her way over to me with cautious, measured steps, concerned at how I was staring off into space, not speaking and probably not breathing very much.

"Are you...okay?" She asked carefully, not sure what was happening, exactly.

"I don't actually know." I replied.

To her credit Maggie let there be a silence between us and she let me be the one to fill it. Talking is hard when you are in so much pain.

"I landed on my hip, and I don't know if I can move it yet. I am just gonna chill here."

Maggie nodded and walked away to collect Toby, who had parked himself in the corner or the arena, far, far, from the scene of the crime. She took her time getting him and made her way back to us, without haste. I was glad for this lack of urgency, because I just needed to process, unfortunately feel, and simply sit there. I must have been there for five minutes, staring into the abyss, and wondering when a good time to try getting up would be, if I even could. Just when I was about to try, Maggie prompted,

"Do you think you could get up?"

"I'll try now, I guess." I wasn't really all that sure, but the first step was to bend my joints around.

Surprisingly I was still upright, torso still in the air and legs out in front of me as if I was causally sitting down. I landed on the right hip, so I wiggled my right ankle a little bit to see if my leg would get worse with movement, or if it even could move it at all. The ankle roll was fine so I bent my knee up so my foot was lying flat on the ground now, a little stiff, but I could do it. *Whew... nothing broken, I think. I was getting worried there.*

I extended the leg out again and folded it back a few times with no difference, the kicker would be if I could put weight on it. I propped myself up with my hands, placing the good left foot first, still holding the right one up off the ground. Just as I did with Toby, I slowly extended that leg down and progressively loaded my weight on it until I was able to stand. Some deep breaths and acceptance of the throbbing that still radiated from my hip, I hobbled around a few steps. I had a bit of a limp, but it felt like it would stretch out and go away if I kept walking on it.

I looked at Maggie and offered my hand outward for the lead rope. She obliged and gave me Toby back.

"Sorry Toby, we won't do that again." His expression was still hidden under the forelock, but he did sneeze at this moment. I think we understood each other. Or at least he understood that he wasn't going to be ridden again, and could do something about it if anyone tried.

I limped back to the pasture and turned Toby out, shocked that the worst fall I have had yet, the worst pain, was due to a fall from a mini. Humbling to say the least.
Toby took off running, farting and bucking once I released him into the field, confidence overcoming him now.
That will do Toby, that will do.

~

Is It Broke? did continue though, just not on minis. This one woman came by with these two small Welsh ponies that she wanted her kids to ride. The problem was, she knew nothing about horses, nor did her kids, and they didn't have any money for training, only the board for the ponies, who were small enough that they could rent one stall and share it.

The Cowboy found a solution to this and suggested that Maggie and I could train the ponies, for free. We of course didn't care, we just wanted to ride. The Cowboy told us that the ponies had about half a dozen rides on them and to go from there. We were excited for the opportunity and we each picked a pony, I chose the orange sorrel named Twinkle, and Maggie picked the bay named Star. Not very creative names but the little girls picked them. Both were mares, very sweet, and incredibly petite. We were used to Quarter Horses and warmblood crosses, these ponies were delicate, almost spider like. I was a bit concerned that I wouldn't have anything to grip on as they had no barrel to wrap my legs around to speak of. Same problem on the minis really, only the ponies were tall enough for us to ride, just quite narrow.

When we went to ride them, we discovered we didn't have any tack that fit them. Our saddle pads were too big, girths too long, and our bridles and bits way too big as well. Oddly enough our English saddles seemed to be ok.

There was a bin of stuff that people left over the years, and we were able to fish out smaller girths from there. Although they were still too big, they were better than what we had for our full-size horses, which would have never fit even on the final holes. We settled on half pads for saddle pads, as they only went under the saddle and wouldn't be flapping about everywhere. We didn't have a solution for the bits or the bridles so we just used full cheek bits that were too big. Because of the design, which had upright spindles on the sides, we couldn't pull the bit through their mouth. This was the best solution we could think of, although not ideal. For bridles we took a piece of bailing twine, tied it to one end of the bit, looped it over the back of their ears, and tied off to the bit again on the other side.

"This is so hillbilly!" Maggie said with a laugh.

"Yep... but what choice do we have? We have to get these horses rode. We will tell the lady she has to buy different tack when we see her next."

Since they had already been ridden, we did a few basic checks on the ground and hopped on. We put a good ride on them too, walk, trot, and canter, both directions. The ponies were a little on the lazier side but listened and gave us no trouble at all. We were very pleased with our efforts, and made a report to The Cowboy about how the horses would probably be ready for their less experienced kids, sooner, rather than later.

The Cowboy seemed confused.

"Wait, so you both rode the bay one?"
We looked at each other, equally confused. Why would he think that?

"No, she rode the bay and I rode the sorrel."

He was taken aback by this and almost looked mad, but then it changed to looking a little proud,

"That sorrel has never been ridden; the bay is the one that has a few rides on it."

We gave each other a sideways look. We were shocked. I had ridden this poor horse for over an hour, putting her through all the paces on her first ride. No ground work, no tack introductions. I still didn't know if I believed that, but I guess I would take the credit.

"Are you sure?" I wasn't buying it; the pony was too good. If it was true then she was one of the ones that they call "born broke."

"Yep, sure am," The Cowboy replied. "That is what the lady said, and they are only three years old, too."

"Oh geez, I feel bad now," I said, embarrassed and looking down at the ground.

Up until now *Is it broke? had been* about finding out what to do with the horse. Since they always ended up being broke, I didn't think of it as being unkind to the horse, just risky for us. But starting young horses was something else entirely, and a topic I took seriously with Vador and Little Q. At the time it wasn't the same thing in my head. I felt awful for subjecting poor Twinkle to this stupidity, I would have never done that had I known.

"Well don't feel too bad, she is broke now and she wasn't yesterday." He seemed somewhat relieved that I was able to get this done, that his plan had worked in a roundabout way, and he wouldn't have to do it now.

I gave a small smile, still feeling bad, and starting to question the ethics of our little game.

I loved riding young horses and never wanted to make a mistake in their training. I also wanted to make it enjoyable for them. Why was I willing to throw out all those principles on a horse I thought was broke?

I vowed I would never do something like this ever again.

Well, almost never again, I still needed to use this hillbilly set up until the owner bought something else for us to use.

Railroad Crossing

Pippin, the poor abandoned horse at the barn came out of *Is it broke?* with nothing to write home about, in many ways was a really great horse. Maggie had taken to riding her for Helen, and Pippin even went on our cider mill ride. The whole barn, and I mean virtually every single person, whether this was the only time of year they rode or not, would ride their horses the six or so miles down the road to the local cider mill and back. As you can image, thirty horses going along down the road was quite a sight, and we had ground people to help stop traffic for us at road crossings. Pippin handled all the energy and all the horses well, and she became a favorite for us to take trail riding.

On a day where nothing in particular happened, and there wasn't anything to talk about or anything out of the ordinary, we made our way back from our trail ride in the back and started to cross the railroad tracks.

I was on Flash, one of Helen's ponies, and Maggie on Pippin. Flash went first and picked his feet high to avoid the black hole that was the gaps between the rail road ties, the train railing, and the wood the filled in the space between them to allow a car to drive over, and the train to still operate. It was basically a pseudo-bridge over the tracks. This was flatter, and we always crossed this way, although many horses protested about it. We could have skipped the crossing and just gone on the tracks themselves, which would have been more inviting to the horses. But the way to get to them was very sloped and the gravel easily gave way en route, so we would be trading one problem for another. The crossing was the lesser of two evils.

Maggie and Pippin were close behind me. Before we crossed, we listened for trains, knowing if we even remotely heard one it would be upon us in under a minute, at top speed, too. We never wanted to mess around with the train so we waited for silence to cross, then did so quickly.

You could hear the echo of the horse's hooves over the wood, *clip, clop, clip, clop,* but behind me all I heard was, *clip, clop, clip...* and then nothing. Before I could turn around, I heard another sign of trouble,

"What the!"

I turned around to see Maggie in the middle of the crossing but one of Pippin's hind feet was STUCK in between the rail and the wood. There had to be a gap between the two so the train could use the railings it ran on, and the gap is maybe about the size of a grown person's fist across. Pippin's foot had gone straight down at the toe and her hoof was wedged between her heel bulb and the rail.

"You're stuck," I told her, a little shaky. I realized what this meant. This was serious.

"What do you mean, stuck?" She was almost angry; horses can't get stuck in railroad tracks. Can they?
I needed to be calm, but she needed to get off. I took a deep breath and lowered my energy,

"Get off. Get off now." Maggie did get off, and went to looking at that left back leg that never made it over.

Immediately our minds went to the trains. To the south you would be able to see the train coming, but on the North side the tracks were curved in such a way that if you saw it, it would be right there a second later. The train always whistled as it crossed, and there was another crossing on a dirt road about a half mile north of here, which could give us a little heads up. We didn't see or hear anything but it was only a matter of time. Trains went by here sometimes ten times a day. Pippin needed to get out of there. I tied Flash's reins to the saddle pad and lead him to a grass patch that was firmly on the side of the tracks by the barn. He started munching on grass with no care for Pippin or her predicament. *Good, if he wants to go back, he can and he will be safe. Someone will see my tacked horse and come for us.*

We didn't have our phones, and there wasn't time to run back, if we did the train might come, we were going to have to get her unstuck and fast. Pippin was trying to get her foot unstuck, but seeing that it wasn't going to work she didn't panic or put too much effort into it. That was good because Maggie grabbed ahold of her leg, just below the hock, and I grabbed her fetlock as we planned to pull upward as hard as we could.

Panic in our eyes as we both knew what would happen if we couldn't get Pippin free, but we had to try.

"Ok…" I took a deep breath, "One, Two, THREE!" We yanked up with all our might, but could not get her leg to budge.

"Try jerking it up," Maggie suggested.
We tried jerking it rhythmically instead of the continuous pull. Nothing.

"Can we push it sideways?" I asked, maybe we could get her free by sliding her out. We pushed it to the right because it was pinched a little on the left. It moved a little but under a half inch, not enough to push it clear off the tracks.

"Is there a crow bar or something we could pry the wood back with?" Maggie asked as she searched around the crossing for something. There were some signs in the gravel, but they were deep and set in, not worth using our strength over.

"Errrrrr…" we turned our heads to the South and thought we heard something, faint, but we couldn't see anything. Maybe we just imagined it?

We looked at each other with the most desperate of looks, how would we get out of this? How would Pippin?

We would try and run for help but there weren't many people at the barn today, and what if we wasted time? A horrible, sinking feeling of helplessness and impending doom flooded my head. There was nothing we could do. Nothing! I couldn't help it, but I started envisioning what it would look like if a horse got hit by a train. We would have to stand there and watch it happen. I couldn't bear that, but what else could we do!

But, wait…

I suddenly remembered that I had a knife in my pocket. I knelt down to Pippin's stuck foot and felt around with my fingers. The part she was stuck on was porous, I had seen the farrier cut it off before. Her hoof was stuck higher than what I had seen him cut, but I felt it again to be sure and it was squishy. She really was only stuck here, if I could cut a bit away, she could be free. At any rate it was better than getting hit by a train.

"I can cut this," I said, looking up at Maggie," And then I think she can get free!"
She wrinkled her nose in disgust but came down to the hoof to investigate and see what I meant.
She took a deep breath when she saw what I saw and stood up and walked to Pippin's head, stroking it. The poor horse didn't know what was coming.

"Do it," she said with all the resolve she could muster.

I wasn't looking for a gory solution to this problem, but I saw no other way. I stood slightly in front of Pippin's leg so that when it got free, she wouldn't' be able to kick me right away, as I would if someone cut off a part of my foot. The hoof itself doesn't hurt when it is trimmed and cut, but this was the heel bulb, and this had blood vessels.

I swallowed hard as I got my knife out, my pocket knife I used to cut hay strings, and lined the blade up to the piece the was stuck. I wanted to cut as little as possible, but not cut so little that I ended up cutting more times than I needed to. I pressed the blade close to the stuck point and pointed it up and pressed in and down, sawing up.

Pippin must have been used to all the pressure the track was exerting on her foot because she didn't really move. It did bleed as I cut, but thankfully not so much that I couldn't see what I was doing. I went up until I got just about to the skin, then took the knife and tapered it inward, more toward the rail and the point it was stuck at, trying to get under it. Once I started the curved portion, I felt a bit if a release by her foot and I asked Maggie to pull on it again.

"ONE, TWO, THREE!" We pulled with all our might, and toward the end of our strength we felt the leg move up a bit.

"ALMOST THERE!" I grunted, out of breath and praying this would work.

The hoof gave way, tearing as it did and widening the part I had scalped, sliced away now and sticking out straight about the size of a pinky finger. We walked Pippin over the rest of the track, terrified that she would put her hoof in the other gap ahead. She didn't, although I would have been happier if she had lifted her leg higher.

"That actually worked!" Maggie was in disbelief.

"I am glad it did... could you imagine?"

"I don't want to think about it," she cut me off and we walked in silence back to the barn.

Amazingly, Pippin wasn't limping and didn't seem to bothered by her near-death experience. I mean, we knew what could happen but she didn't.

Maggie did eventually break the silence with a new edict,

"Every time we cross those tracks from now on, we are getting off and leading them across. It's not worth it, that could happen again."

I thought about it for a moment, irritated that we would have one more thing to do, but I knew she was right, it could happen again and we might not be so lucky.

"Yeah, you're right, we can get off and lead them from now on."

An odd thought occurred to me as I agreed with her: Did we just grow up? Did we just make our own rule?

I didn't say this out loud but Maggie seemed to hear me and gave me a confirming look that said, *yes, we know better now.*

Two Versions of a Head-to-Head Barrel Race

Part 1: "It's Gonna be a Horse Race!"

    Little Q got better at barrel racing, and stronger too. Her stifle didn't lock up quite as much, but we had yet to take her to a competition and see how she would hold up. There was a big gymkhana day at Hilltop, so the cowboys loaded up their young horses to ride around, and let me tag along to compete. It was only a twenty-minute ride from the barn so there wasn't a ton of time to mentally prepare.

    There especially wasn't time to prepare for what I saw when I opened the trailer door. Q was in the first compartment of the slant load trailer, which was unloaded last. And thank goodness because as I pushed the metal partition away and walked toward Q's head, I saw a three-legged horse.

    Q's left leg was stuck forward, higher than her shoulder, *inside* the hay bag! The hay bag was a thin, webbed, rope sack that was filled at the top and then pulled shut. The hay bags were cheap, only a few dollars, but the holes were obviously big enough to catch a hoof. She must have been pawing impatiently, or reared up in the trailer at some point to be in this predicament.

    Q turned her head toward me and gave me a *help me* look. What on earth would I do?

I walked closer to her, trying to examine exactly how she was caught. Her hoof had gone completely through one of the holes and was inside the bag up to her fetlock. We couldn't back up, if she tried to back up and felt the room to do so, she could panic and pull back hard, potentially slicing her leg open with the thin nylon. I couldn't pull her leg down and I really couldn't pick it up, it was locked at the end of its ability to extend and held way higher than a hoof should have been. I looked up toward where the bag was tied, but it wasn't attached to a clip, it was tied up to the welded tie rings itself. The force of a horse leaning on it had completely sealed off the knot, making it impossible to untie. I would have to cut her free, but of course I didn't have a knife.
I called for the Cowboys, anyone.

"HELP! I NEED A KNIFE!" I hoped someone would come to my aid, I couldn't leave Q, but I couldn't get her free either. What if she had already injured herself badly? There wasn't any blood, but tendon injuries can be insidious. I would know more once I got her out of here and she started to walk.

The Quiet One came around the corner of the trailer, knife in hand. I was happy he took my word for it, and didn't ask questions, just ready to help. He crept partially into the trailer to hand me the knife, but moved slowly and steadily, aiding but not adding to the energy.
His centeredness was well placed because as I backed away from Q's head, she started to panic, flail, and reared, taking her other front leg off the ground in protest of me leaving her side. *No don't go! Help!* She seemed to say.

"EAAAAAAASSSSSYYYYY," The Quiet One slowly bellowed in a deep baritone, trying to quiet the mare. But he didn't step forward, he just kept his arm extended the same way it was, as I took the knife from him, and slinked back toward Q.

There wasn't more than two feet of space in between me and her, and she needed to stop rearing and stay still so I could cut her out.

"Heeeey," I breathed out to soothe her. I entered into her space, the small, tight, unpredictable space that held danger for me if she chose to panic. But what other choice do we have but to enter the danger when it is called upon us? We can't give it to others, it is ours. We can only step forward, lower the energy, and in many ways surrender ourselves to fate. To the horse. For there is no other choice.

I inched slowly forward as Q got herself back to three feet on the ground but was swaying from side to side, rocking the trailer as she did.

"Heeeyyy," I breathed again, and reached my hand to her shoulder to give her a comforting touch.
She settled a bit. I moved my hand up to her neck, stroking first lightly to soothe, then firmly to add confidence.

Q continued to breathe hard but stopped, surrendering herself to me for a moment, understanding I could help. I kept an eye on her head as I raised the knife. Her ears flickered a bit towards me but she didn't look like she was going blow up again, so I started cutting.

The cuts needed to be above where all her weight was and to the side so I could hopefully just push it over. Cutting below held too much a risk of cutting her in the process, or more likely she would move as she felt the pressure release, trying to get free too early.

Each cut I breathed out a bit, trying to keep my heart rate down and steady so as not to provoke a panic from Q. She stood still as I cut, seeming to understand. Also, I am sure she was exhausted. Who knows how long she had been stuck that way before I could come to her aid?

Once all the cuts were done, I reached deep inside the bag and pulled her leg toward me and the hole I had made. It slid through relatively easy, and Q slammed her hoof to the ground once she knew she was free. Then let out a big sneeze and a sigh, releasing all the tension she had in her.

We stood there for a moment, and stayed calm in each other's presence. Once Q started munching on the hay that had dropped to the floor from the hay bag, I knew it was time to back out and assess the damage.

Q backed out of the trailer a little hurried, as if she suddenly remembered what had happened. Seeing the hustle and bustle of a horse show, she immediately began prancing around on the end of her lead, taking everything in.

"Go walk her around a bit," The Quiet One instructed.

"Well, she looks, okay?" I asked more as a question than a statement.

"You won't know until she calms down…that's the adrenaline of being in a new spot. She could run a race right now and still be lame. We will see how she is in about twenty minutes." As he said this, he walked away to take care of his horses.

I wanted to compete today of course, but I really wanted Q to be ok and uninjured from the trip. I was happy that The Quiet One had let me fix it, instead of just shoving me away so he could. *I must be getting better; he had enough faith in me to fix this myself.*

Despite the situation, that was a comforting thought. More comforting still was Q had let me help her. She got upset when I left. She trusted me enough to get her out of the bind she was in. Competition or no competition, I had insight into a true bond I had developed with this horse. This was something to be treasured, and while I couldn't comprehend all of the intricacies of it, I knew that it was special.

Q calmed down in a few minutes and her gait seemed to be fine. She wasn't limping, short stepping, or twisting at all when she stepped. I stopped and let her eat grass and massaged her shoulder and forearm muscle on that side to see if they were sore, but they weren't. Her tendon wasn't swollen or hot. Her pastern, which was where she was truly stuck at, just had a little hair rubbed off, but no blood, cuts, or gashes.

Upon my return I informed The Quiet One of my inspections and my opinion on how Q was. He repeated the same things I did and made me lunge her in front of him before saying,

"She looks fine, she can show," with a subtle smile on his face. When he said nothing, it was a compliment, he liked how I handled everything.

The chaos over, we entered Q in pretty much all the events: barrels, flags, keyhole, speed and action, and head-to-head barrels. I had practiced all the others ones at length but had never done the head-to-head.

"It's a race!" The Cowboy explained, "You have two different barrel patterns, one on each end of the ring, and you both start in the middle, facing different directions. You both run your own pattern, and the first over the finish line wins!" That sounded easy enough. But he continued,

"It is a bracket, so if you win, you keep going against other people that won; if you lose you go against other people that lose until there is an ultimate winner. The winner actually runs and wins the most."

"So how many times will I run?" I asked, confused.

"That depends how much you win!" he said with a chuckle, walking away.

The Cowboy seemed most excited about the head-to-head because that was how he'd won some of his world titles on the Appaloosa circuit twenty years prior. A lot of the speed events were run in that bracket system back then. He wanted to see history repeat itself.

I had plenty of time to get my feet wet because the head-to-head was the last event of the day.

When barrels came, the first event of the day, I was a little nervous, and messed that up, going way too wide on the first, earning a twenty second pattern, not good enough to place. Next was flags, I completely missed the flag on the pickup. Nerves.

Keyhole is when it finally started to turn around. In keyhole they use flour to make the shape of a "key," a medium circle that has two parallel lines at the entrance, barely a horse length in width, forming an alley into the circle. The goal is to run through the lines, into the circle, then turn around and run back through the lines all without ever stepping on or outside of the flour. Fastest time that doesn't disqualify, wins.

I let Q run at a medium pace towards the key, keeping her right in the middle of the corridor and going as far into the key as I could before sitting down and turning my head toward the opening again. Q set back on her powerful haunches and lifted her shoulder around, almost rearing, to spin completely around. I didn't urge her faster until I knew we were straight in between the lines and then I raced her on with all I could, and she was happy to give it to me. We sprinted across the timer to hear the time of 11.645 boom across the speakers. I looked up from the crowd to see The Cowboy clapping and hooting from outside the pen, a rare sight.

The Speed and Action event was next. There is a small, just over horse-length flour-lined box that you run through down to the other end of the arena where there are three cones. You have to turn around the center cone while keeping the other cones to your outside, race back towards the box, and stop in it. You have to stay in the box until the judge, who is standing right there watching the flour lines, dismisses you. Knock the cones down, don't stay to inside of the border cones, or step on or over the flour lines and you are out. Fastest clean time wins.

Q had pretty good brakes so I felt like I could really push this one. I ran through the box and down to those cones without hesitation. I knew you had to run a little past all of the cones before you whipped around to give you "mess up room" if you needed it. Q passed that center cone, and once her hind legs were clear of it, I sat down and snapped my head around, and she complied by lowering her hocks into the ground spinning around, easy and cat-like. We passed through the cones easily and about a stride before the box I sat down and yelled,

"WHOA!"

Q sat back down and easily and came to stop, tapping her feet in place ready to run again, but obedient and trotting on the spot, waiting.

The judge gave the thumbs up and I relaxed to give Q a hug in the neck as she trotted out of the box while a time of 9.887. Good enough for second place! The Cowboy was elated. This kid was finding her groove.

I walked Q for a good twenty minutes and brought her back to the trailer for some water and hay before the head-to-head race, when The Cowboy made a point to talk to me about strategy.

"Ok Munchkin... this is how this works..." he had a glint in his eye, proud that he could share this knowledge with me. I looked up at him, a man who was essentially my dad, ready to tell me how to make this work. He could barely contain his excitement. It was my turn now, I got to experience the giddiness that came out of him when one of his students was doing well. He continued in a hurried voice,

"They are going to have a chalk line that is the start and stop line in the middle of the ring, and they are gonna call out 'Ready, set, go!' but you can't cross over the line until they say 'go'." He dropped his chin and gave me a serious look to check in and made sure I got it, he didn't have to say it, but I knew that if I went over the line before they said "go" I would be disqualified, and there would be line judges standing right there to verify.

"You will be facing different ways but passing by each other like cars on the highway. You run your separate pattern, and then you will run at each other towards the finish line and whoever gets there first wins. It might even be by a nose!" He did a little shake at the prospect of a photo finish but then suddenly remembered a crucial housekeeping detail,

"Oh! Make sure you don't hit the other person at the end! You will be running right towards each other and... ya know... you don't wanna hit!"

The way he had said it made me feel like he had indeed seen people collide in this manner, which was a little terrifying. Of course, I nodded in agreement, obviously, I didn't want to hit anyone. Satisfied with my acknowledgement of risk he continued,

"So...you can't cross that line before they say go, but that doesn't mean you can't be moving before they do..."

There was that glint in his eye again, I could tell this was not common knowledge that he was about to bestow upon me. I leaned in a little closer to catch all of it.

"Be pretty far back and start running when they say 'ready,' but just don't cross the line till after 'go.' You have to time it just right. But if you do, you'll be running by the time they say 'go,' and the other rider will be starting from a standstill. There is no rule that says you have to be right by the line or starting from a halt. So...strategy."

This made perfect sense and I was pretty sure was something I could pull off. I kept looking at The Cowboy, hoping he would say more,

"Now the rest of the pattern you ride the same, don't spend too much time looking at the other rider, but when you round that third barrel, find them so you know how hard you have to run home-if you really have to punch it, or you'll be able to win anyway and save your horse for the next race. This is really a game of who is smarter and also fast, not necessarily who is the fastest."

I liked that. If I could use my brain to win just as much as my horse's speed, I stood a better chance than someone who was purely faster than me. I had been showing for a while now, and I had learned a lot about strategy, but up until now, strategy only mattered if you were really good and so were your competitors. This felt different, strategy was at the forefront. It was a new territory.

When it was time to go in, I was matched with someone who was decently fast and I had seen compete earlier that day. They had certainly had a better barrel pattern than I did before. But...this time maybe I could out strategize them. I picked the south facing direction and my competitor, on a big bay, lined up facing north. I could see him line right up at the line. I confidently trotted a good five strides or so back from where they were and looked right at the judge to confirm that I was where I wanted to be. I saw my competitor give a little smirk as he saw how far back I was, but I kept a poker face. They didn't know what I did. A nod from each of us locked us in.

"Get ready!" I was already ready.

"Get set!" I started trotting towards the start line and asked for a canter in the gap of time between commands. My competitor saw what I was doing but was powerless to stop it because he was right on the line.

"Go!" I was already in a bit of a run as the line judge said "go" a foot or so before I passed it. I had done it! I turned my first barrel to the right with such delight that I had played the game well, and cruised towards the second, left hand turn, as the bay horse was just starting to turn the first turn. Yes!

I kept my pace, turned the second and headed to the third. They were behind me now, and I couldn't see them but they would be no doubt trying to catch me. A nice third left hand turn again and I was heading back for the line as they were still heading for their third barrel. I coasted to the finish line, before they got done turning their third. Victory!

I felt a little bad for the other rider, but this was a game of strategy, there were no rules against it. What an odd sensation this was, to think my way through the ride, and I didn't have to use up my horse too much at the end, so she was fresher for the next go around.

My next competitor had seen what I had done and tried to replicate it, but didn't have the timing right, and ended up pulling up on "set" because they were too close to the line, botching their momentum.

The next one started from too far back and was running by the time the judge yelled "Go!" but they still had three more strides to go before the start line.

The next one had the timing figured out, and matched my start, but pushed her horse too fast in an attempt to beat me, sending her too wide and too far past the first barrel, wasting precious time and allowing me to make it up with a more correct pattern.

Strategy was winning.

I knew I would place by how the bracket was going along, and I hadn't lost yet, but my next competitor was someone to worry about. I didn't know the rider but I knew the horse: a white Arabian mare named China. China had won a lot of events, and was smooth as butter. Her rider also was equally smooth and poised. She would be able to match my timing, and she wouldn't get too excited or push too hard and blow it. Our strategy and composure would match, it would come down to the speed.

China's rider didn't look at me, but she put herself a little farther back than I would have. She was going to try and beat me at my own game.
Bring it.
I went about the same distance and nodded to the judge, locking eyes with China's head. I wasn't moving until she was. We would bolt together.

"Get Ready!" On the "Y" of "ready" China leapt forward and I followed suit.

"Get Set!" We were about three strides away the two of us, still pushing.

"Go!" and on the "O" of "go" we were both across that line heading towards our respective first barrels.

I was proud of myself, but I couldn't help but be impressed by China's rider as well. It was a merging of minds for a few glorious moments, a synergy that sent a bolt of energy into my legs as I chased Q on towards the second barrel. We were running in lockstep as we entered the turn together. I couldn't see her when we left the second, and I needed to focus on turning the third correctly, but I knew we were together, I just hoped it would stay. Before I picked up my eyes from the third, before I could find her and gauge how hard I needed to run I heard The Cowboy growl out in a gruff voice,

"IT'S GONNA BE A HORSE RACE!" I knew that it was going to come down to that final stretch running towards the line; we would have to give it everything we had.

As soon as we were clear of the barrel I got up on Q's neck and grabbed some mane, kept my head down and kicked every stride hissing and urging Q on. Q complied with dropping her head, perking her ears forward, grabbing the earth with her front legs and charging onward, reaching farther, pushing harder, she gave it her all and then some I didn't know she had.

It was perfect.

China was barreling straight at us, but she had a little more to give than Q, and Q was truly giving her best. I didn't let up, but in the last stride, I knew China would overtake us. We crossed that line, almost together, but China's delicate black nose poked out about a foot more than Q's. I had lost but I had lost to an equal. I was actually pretty ecstatic. When we pulled up and headed back to the line for them to formally announce the winner, I looked over at China's rider to congratulate her, but before I could she told me,

"Good run...real good run," with a nod as her horse pranced around from under her. I wanted to say 'thank you' and 'likewise', but she was already gone.

When I got out of the ring you would have thought I did win because The Cowboy gave me a huge hug as soon as I got off Q.

"That was so awesome! You were incredible! What a treat to watch!"

He wrapped me up in his arms with the kind of embrace a father should give a daughter, firm, and protecting, but light enough not to crush. He picked me up off the ground a little bit and spun me around with joy. It was everything I could have ever wanted.

"You are going places, Munchkin. That was incredible!" I held back a tear in eyes as I hugged him again.

"Thanks for teaching me!" I choked out.

He melted a little at this and gave me still another hug. I had made him proud. It was one of the only times I had made someone truly proud. I had accomplished something that was taught, and I had lived up to expectations. I did something worth of praise. The Cowboy's praise, which didn't come easy. Even The Quiet One had cheered and clapped while I rode, and I got a, "great job kiddo, that was impressive," more words than he usually said in a day.

Q and I barrel racing.

Part Two: Knocked-Off Boots

As the Cowboy's students grew in number and became more advanced, we started heading out to Hilltop on weeknights during the summer and practiced there. Since the group was usually over ten people, the lesson would go into the two-hour mark. I, of course, trailered over with him, so we were first there and the last to leave. The group was very dedicated, some driving over an hour to attend. Sometimes, people even brought dinner for everyone. The Cowboy had turned these group lessons into kind of team practice and people treated it as such. Everyone wanted to be there and learn from him, not just because he was good and produced winners, not just because he had won some world titles himself, but because he made you feel a part of something.

You're with us, this is home. This is home.

To me, it was. The sand swirling in the air, the squeak of leather as people trotted by, the breath of horses exhaling rhythmically galloping between the barrels, the sun setting over that huge hill we had to walk up one hundred times.

My friends...The Cowboy...The Quiet One... my hands on the reins.

This is home.

I was on my third horse now, a four-year-old tank of a grey gelding named Mo. Mo was off the track, the Quarter Horse track, where they only sprint a quarter-mile or less, and he was the most powerful horse I had ridden to date. I was able to buy him and a Western saddle with the sale of Vador, who was well known locally and I was able to sell him for top-dollar.

I had switched from English to Western. My friends joking called it "going to the dark side."

Although truly multi-discipline trainers, The Cowboy and The Quiet One were, at the end of the day, more Western than English. I had gone about as far as I was going to go with them in jumping. I was doing 2'6-2'9 courses and the occasional 3' jump, but if I was going to continue down that path, I would need to leave Wind Row and go to a hunter barn to do it. I would have to leave the men who became my dads to reach higher heights myself.

The choice was easy: Stay with them. Stay home.

I would have loved to have kept racing on Q as well, but it was no longer in her best interest. Q's stifle problems only intensified the more that she ran, and she would need an expensive procedure to correct it. I could no longer bear it when her stifle locked, her leg dragging behind her, the pitiful face she made knowing she couldn't move. *Help me* she said with those eyes, knowing I always would as I had before. I kept backing her up until the stifle popped back into place. To paraphrase the old saying, "the spirit was willing but the flesh was weak."

By that time, she was a finished riding horse. Helen or someone else could ride her, I just didn't want to race her anymore. The horse came first.

The Cowboy convinced me to get a younger horse and train it to do barrels myself. This horse, however, would be a quality prospect and very athletic, with excellent breeding. And Mo was. He was by a top producing stud on the Quarter horse track, and was beautifully built, well-muscled, and fast. His worst day was Q's best day in terms of the power he could push through a turn. We were all excited about what he would be able to do.

That being said, we were taking it slow, and at this point had not entered him in a race yet. We were just getting him off the property, and this group setting was a great experience for him to get some miles. When I'd bought him, it had only been three weeks since his last race. Needless to say, I had my work cut out for me, but overall, we were doing well. But this particular story isn't about me, it's what happened to Tom and Ashley.

Tom was a tall, slim guy with darker, almost Latin features, even though that wasn't his heritage. He and his brother took lessons from The Cowboy, and Tom was very into it, and very into doing well. He was so focused he didn't talk to a lot of people in the group. I tried to get his Myspace URL a few times and he eventually gave it to me, under duress, and was completely disinterested in being friends. He had real cowboy-style horse, King, who was a solid bay gelding, devoid of any white. King was all business, just like his owner.

Ashley was on a collegiate equestrian team with Tom, and I was friends with her. She was loud, boisterous, and fearless. I loved hanging around her. Her horse was a bit of a hothead, a slender black mixed-breed named Athena. I remember that Athena liked to rear quite a bit when she wanted to go, and Ashley rode it with ease and style. A girl after my own heart. No wonder we were friends.

The Cowboy had been jazzed up about the head-to-head barrel race that I competed in last year, and he wanted to have everyone try it. Some of us had done it over the winter back at Wind Row, but we couldn't really go full out in that arena.

Tom and Ashley hadn't done it yet so they were eager to go first. Since they were about the same skill level, The Cowboy thought they would be a good match for each other, and it would be a visually entertaining spectacle for all the parents sitting on the hill watching the lesson. My money was on Ashley, solely because I knew her and how competitive she was. Tom was pretty stoic, so I couldn't gauge him, and I didn't really care, frankly.

The Cowboy explained the rules to everyone, but we had all heard it before so we just politely listened again. *Come on…let's get to it!* We got it, we got it, time to run.

The Cowboy set up cones where the finish line would be, and all of us extras exited the ring to watch from the outside so Tom and Ashley could have full use of the arena.

"On your mark," The Cowboy had a big smile on his face, this was going to be good!

"Get set," he dropped his voice a little bit to steady himself.

"Go!" he yelled and jumped up into the air as he did, yelling about an octave higher. This was his thing, and he was passing it on, to the next generation.

Tom and Ashley didn't disappoint as they charged their horses forward, I knew Ashley would mean business but I was surprised at how much Tom urged King on to beat her.

But trouble started as soon as they left.

Ashley went to the left barrel first.

When you do head-to-head barrels, both people go to the right first, as most people do while running barrels anyway. You start facing the other rider, and run towards them but in your own lane. Since you both are turning to your own right, you won't run into each other while on pattern. Except Ashley went to the left barrel first.

Since neither Ashley nor Tom had ever done head-to-head barrels, they didn't think of it as a problem. Both thought they were racing to their respective barrels, and they were, they just didn't count on their paths intersecting. At top speed. With tunnel vision, focused on trying to win.

The Cowboy noticed the error immediately and started screaming,

"WATCH OUT WATCH OUT WATCH OUT!!!!"

But they couldn't hear him, going that fast, hearing is one of the first senses to go. While running the focus is on flying ahead, the senses narrowing on what's forward, not what is to the side or behind.

They never saw it coming. Their horses didn't either, fully committed to running to that first barrel. I stood there aghast on the sidelines watching them about to obliterate each other, and there was nothing I could do.

It sounded like a car crash.

A crunching thud and a boom echoed out across the arena. The horses hit, shoulder to shoulder, without even a hint of slowing down. One-thousand-pound animals colliding at forty miles an hour. The impact caused Ashley's horse to buckle and fall, tossing Ashley out to the side and under her mount. Tom's horse King buckled his front legs a bit on impact and stumbled over Athena's legs that were now on the ground, ejecting Tom off to the other side, hard, before succumbing to gravity, a flurry of sand billowing around him as he nosedived into the dirt.

I might have just seen them die.

A blood curdling scream filled the echo of the impact.

"NOOO!!!" It was Ashley's dad, running from the hill across the arena to come to the aid of his fallen daughter, whose horse was still pinning her to the ground.

Everyone was on the ground, and no one was moving.

The Cowboy was white as a ghost and started running too, but to Tom. One of the other girl's mom was a nurse, and she quickly, but more calmy jogged her way into the arena to evaluate the injuries. Everyone else took a step closer to the fencing.

All of the activity caused Athena to stir and get up. I was worried that she would step on Ashley as she scrambled to her feet, but she was able to pick her feet up and around her rider despite the scrambling. Ashley still lay on the ground as her dad crouched next to her. The nurse went there first. Tom started coughing and hacking up the dirt that had gone into his mouth. By this time his dad had joined the group in the arena, but he entered at a brisk walk. I got the feeling this was not the most dramatic thing he had seen. Tom got up a bit onto his elbows and kept coughing.

Why would he cough? I didn't understand why he would keep doing that unless he hurt his lung or inhaled dirt. The more I thought about it, those scenarios actually seemed pretty likely.

Tom eventually got up and when he did, I saw to my absolute amazement that he no longer had his cowboy boots on.

They had hit so hard that his boots had been knocked off.

I had never seen anything like that. Tom seemed to notice it himself, looking down and chuckling a bit in between coughs, as he limped over to his horse, who had since gotten up but stood still as a statue, dazed by his accident.

Ashley did eventually sit up, we later learned that the wind had been knocked out of her, bad, and she just couldn't catch her breath. She had also lost a boot on impact. Why only one is anyone's guess.

Somehow, impossibly, no one was seriously injured, just bruised, embarrassed and shoeless.

The horses were fine as well. Neither suffered any injuries from the impact, but they did pin their ears every time they rode past each other afterward- they must have remembered and held a grudge.

I don't remember the rest of the lesson; I don't remember going home right away but I know for fact that there were no more head-to-head barrels.

-Adult Reflections-

Car crash victims lose shoes on impact.

This is the epitome of "almost." Nothing happened this time, but I have heard plenty of horror stories since:

Stories of horses who fell at a run and their riders that were crushed on impact.

Stories of people whose horses have collided like that, and suffered from heart arrhythmias thereafter.

Stories of collisions and broken backs.

Stories of falls that were a whirl of legs, horse and human, that broke in the fray of the fall.

To me they are just stories, but to some people they were reality, a hospital bill, a funeral.

To Ashley and Tom, the lucky ones, it is just a story and some sandy boots.

Alex Tyson

Horse Pancake

There were a lot of famous names at a big futurity event we went to in Ohio the following spring. One such rider, a tall man with long, brown, seemingly permed hair that went down to his belt caught my attention. The man could ride. I mean really ride. It was poetry in motion. He didn't make any mistakes on the barrel pattern. Not one. I had never seen anyone ride so smoothly and fluid, so perfect. His hands were balanced and soft through the turn, he only moved them exactly as necessary. His pockets (the path that you take around the barrel turn) were perfectly symmetrical, even on both sides of the "U" shaped path. His balance; perfect, he sat back at just the right time, got forward at just the right time.

He had no wasted motion. None. No arm flapping, no star-fishing, no getting a little bit of air time. Nothing. Everything he did, or rather didn't do, was purposeful and meticulously crafted over, I am sure, a number of years. He didn't just ride correctly, stay out of the horse's way, and help the horse when needed; no, he was the horse, or a human extension of one.

People hooted and hollered for five minutes when he broke the arena record that day. He didn't just break it, he smashed it by almost half a second. Excellence is evident when you see it. I could not believe that someone could ride as fast as him and also so classically correct and beautiful.

In barrel racing, the fastest time wins, and often times smooth is fast, but not always. Staying on at fast speeds is a skill all its own; it does not necessarily translate into technical riding ability. There are many ways to ride, and one of those ways is simply getting on and getting the job done, regardless of how it looks or how the horse feels about it. Unfortunately, many barrel racers do this, and they still win, because they have that stay on and get it done mindset. That mindset, arguably, is what settled the West here in the United States, it's the mindset of calvary and military campaigns worldwide. It does, unfortunately, and often times, work to the ends of the user.

But, sometimes, there are people who can transcend this, and show not only how to get it done, but get it done in a way that is kind to the horse, a way that builds a relationship. Something beautiful; not because of an aesthetic, but because of the harmony of man and beast in a synergy that borders on the divine.

I have often thought that God gave humans dominion over animals to give us a glimpse in what it must be like to be him, to care for all humanity. In doing so, we see just how bad we are at it, just how selfish we can really be.

But when we get it right, it feels heavenly. A glimpse into how the world could be.

Seeing that man pilot that horse around at breakneck speed but soft, smooth, and completely in synch was something that I will never forget. It showed what was possible with a horse, and gave me something to strive towards. I want someone to think this way about me one day. I want to ride that well. All horses should have the good fortune of being ridden in this way, or at least with a person who aspires to be that good. As much as we claim to love them, humans do wrong by horses all the time. We care for them poorly, ride poorly, and make bad decisions that affect them in the worst ways.

I was really starting to think about things more critically, *how* I wanted to do something and not just to be able to do it. I had focused on the latter for most of my riding career: be able to jump, gallop, turn barrels, poles, win at a show, ride lots of different horses well, ride bareback, ride double, rides bucks, rears, the list goes on. I was proud of my ability to do those things, but I was starting to have thoughts about why I did some things, why other people did things, and I started asking questions.

    Why use a twisted bit? Why use draw reins to get a horse's head down? Why does that horse looks like it is in pain? Most of my questions got dismissed but I couldn't help but to keep thinking about them. It seemed like something was missing in what I was doing, although I couldn't figure it out. That man with the long hair ignited my musings again, he was doing what I knew I wanted to.

~

    I wanted to do right by Mo at this big show. Mo had gone to expos, or untimed practice runs over the winter, and had been entered a few times, but this time I was really going to ask him to run. This arena was huge by Midwest barrel racing standards, 150X300 with its large metal trusses and thirty foot high ceiling. There was a smaller, older arena attached to the huge one, that served as a warm-up pen and a run-in chute. The whole facility was grand, and made you feel like you had to be somebody, or on your way to being somebody, to run here. Everything about the place was top-notch, except for one seemingly small detail that I just couldn't wrap my head around.

    Horses ran from the warm-up pen, somewhat blind, into the big arena. When the run was done, they ran back into the small arena, but there were no partitions or a space to contain the incoming horse from one building to the next. The riders in the warm-up heard the hooves of the oncoming horse and were expected to move out of the way, but by the time they saw the horse it was too late. Occasionally, a horse ran all the way to the back of the warm-up and used the back wall to stop, dodging kids, dogs, and clueless folks along the way.

This tiny ring, maybe 60X60 had about twenty riders trying to warm-up in it, dodging horses galloping in blindly at breakneck speed.
To say it was chaos would be a gross understatement.

Often there is a chute of some sort for riders to run through; this helps the horse slow down because it sees the gates. The horse stops straight, and is contained until someone lets them out. The partition prevents other horses from colliding with the horse as it is trying to slow down.

Other arenas are set up with a "T" formation, where there is a smaller shoot from the big racing ring to a small holding area. The rider comes out of the racing ring and then has to abruptly go right or left into the holding pen. Other folks are in the holding arena as well, but they are further up the sides and unlikely to get hit.

But here? Just chaos, figure it out.

By this time, I had gotten pretty good at assessing risk and choosing what risks to take. My avoidable wrecks, the ones caused by my stupidity or miscalculations, were behind me. I was sixteen now, and wanted as much as possible to be a mini-adult, so I needed to act like one. Plus, I had learned from a lot of my near misses and considered myself lucky.

This warm-up situation made me reconsider my plan to really open Mo up. Having not run him much, I knew that stopping could be a problem. I didn't really want to run at all now, but I also didn't want to be a chicken. No one, and I mean no one, made any mention of the perilous warm-up arena. They seemed to have no concerns whatsoever about it. I wondered if this was one of those things I still had yet to learn.

I warmed Mo up as much as was possible in the small ring with people zipping in and out of it. I had about fifteen people ahead of me, and I studied every one of them as they pulled up their horses.

Some got lucky, no one was in the way when they flew in, and they easily turned their horse to the right, back towards the opening itself, and pulled up.

Others had to yell "LOOK OUT" as they turned into the other horses that were coming past them, only for their horse to do a bit of a rear at the last second to keep their front legs from smashing into others.

The people who headed straight to the back wall terrified me the most. There were considerably fewer racers choosing this method, and as a result more people tried to congregate their horses at the back of the ring, thinking they'd be out of the way. Riders scrambled away at the last second and flew away from the wall just in time for the incoming horse to almost smash into them.

The main issue here is sight, I thought to myself. People can hear the horse, but they can't see it or where it is going before it is too late. Same with the incoming rider, they can't see that far into the building as they are running into it, and then all the sudden, BOOM! Time to make a decision.

They really just need a chute. This seemed so obvious to me, and so easy to do. It would make everything flow easier, and be safer.

But I was only sixteen, and I knew that I didn't know everything. Perhaps I was missing something here, these people put on shows all the time and I had never done anything like that. Maybe there was a reason that they did it this way that I just didn't know.

*Maybe I need to be braver...*I always felt like I needed to be braver.

I didn't want to let The Cowboy down. I could tell he was excited about the pairing of Mo and me, and what it could do for his reputation. He didn't say anything about the chute; I saw him run earlier, but he was one of the lucky ones who had no one in the way.

Tom was on the sidelines waiting to watch my run, oddly enough, he turned out to be a good guy. Weird, funny, and couldn't care less about what anyone thought about anything. Ever. I didn't like him at first because he ignored me. The feeling was mutual because he thought I was too loud and obnoxious, fake even. But, more recently, he'd started telling jokes, and I started laughing. Then we started talking, riding, warming up together. We weren't dating, but I liked him. He was a real gentleman, someone really born in the wrong era. I am loud and boisterous on the outside, but a calmer, more analytical and calculating person on the inside. Tom was indeed the inside out version of me. He was on the outside what I was on the inside. But he was braver, and arguably (and, unbelievably) more stubborn.

He hadn't thought anything about the warm-up either, and he had already run his horse. He had managed to get King back almost to a lope before he entered the building. Either he wasn't pushing as hard as he should have, or this was his way of dealing with the chaos, by not entering it. I didn't ask him though; we weren't at that stage of our relationship.

He gave me a little smile as the announcer called my name, beckoning me into the ring, but I didn't return it. I was all business when it came to showing, and I had to focus on this large track that lay before me.

I made sure Mo got his right lead before sending him down the alley. As soon as he picked it up, we ran. It must have been 30 strides to the first barrel, and you don't even get to really get a good look until you are almost upon it. The barrel is set pretty close to the wall too, so you had to do it right.

Mo didn't slow down as much as I would have liked and turned the first a little wide, but we still managed to come out straight for the long charge to the second barrel.

Running, running, still running, the run almost seemed to lose its luster as we lumbered on to the second, it was so far away. Normally, a good five to seven strides and you are there. I think we must have gone fifteen.

Mo wrapped the second tight and we carried on, again to what seemed like forever to the third barrel, where Mo turned it okay, but nothing special. He did however run for home; a bit more than I wanted him too. He charged back towards the arena gap and I knew better than to pull, he would just pull harder, but I didn't encourage him either. I just let him coast, galloping at his own pace with no aide from me. A few strides from the timer I asked him to come back, hoping to slow down enough before the warm-up ring and avoid chaos all together, like Tom did.

But Mo didn't come back. He jumped up in the air a bit to avoid my hands and kept charging forward.

Oh no... this is bad.

"Whooooaa" I bellowed in a deep voice that could rival a man's, I was trying to stay calm but I knew this wasn't good, there was no way we could slow down in time.

As the gap came closer Mo slowed a little, but not enough to really matter. We were still at a gallop as we crossed from one arena to the next. The warm-up pen was considerably darker, and it took a moment for my eyes to adjust.

Straight in, towards the back wall were half a dozen riders-so no-go for that stopping plan.
Mo started to drift to the right, which was really the only option. The left was the wall, and at this speed, you would hit it, or rather the horse would whip around and I would hit it. A sea of people was to my right, in the way!

"HEADS UP!" I yelled.

Can't these people get out of the way?!

I had no choice but to turn into them, hoping they would disperse.

Many of them did, with panicked, clueless looks on their faces, as if this was the first time this had ever happened in the history of barrel racing.

But one of them didn't, an older gal on a pinto horse, who I was pretty confident didn't see or hear me. I was going to smash right into her. We were going too fast, her horse was essentially at a standstill, and we would crush him.

I did the only thing I could think to do: I pulled my right rein clear up to my hip in hopes that Mo would wrap his head around and come to a quick stop via a teeny tiny circle in front of the pinto horse, halting my forward motion. I knew this probably wouldn't work but it was a last-ditch effort. I couldn't just sit idly by and let myself, my horse, and this clueless lady get hurt. I had to try, and if I hit them anyway at least I could say I did all I could.

It worked all right, Mo yielded his head to my hand, clear over to my knee, and in doing so killed the engine in the back, and stopped moving forward.

He then promptly lost his balance, slipped his legs clean out from under him, turning him sideways in the air. All four legs had left the ground and my thousand-pound animal landed on his shoulder and skidded to the side, leaving a horse impression in the ground as he slid five feet.
Gasps from the crowd and horrified faces.

"How could this happen?" they seemed to say.
Really?

I managed to keep my head up during the fall but I quickly realized I was pinned under Mo. My right leg was completely under him and my left foot was still in the stirrups, although that leg was almost over his back by this point.

I quickly considered the possibilities: He might be so hurt he can't get up. If he gets up, I need to get my feet free of these stirrups. He could drag me if I am still attached. I had seen in a movie where a horse fell and when he got back up bolted, dragging the jockey who was still attached to one of the stirrups, his foot rotated in a perilous vice. The horse ended up dragging the jockey into a solid object, knocking him free but also knocking him out. That was all I could think of. The guy in the movie shattered his leg. I had to get free.

Mo, thankfully, did not get up immediately, so I was able to kick my left foot free of the stirrup. It was still draped over his side, and it needed to be because of how wide Mo was and the fact that I was pinned down on the other leg. I was free of one stirrup at least, I just had to get the foot from under me free. I would have to wait to do that until he got up, as I couldn't move my leg at the moment. Interestingly enough it didn't hurt, my leg was behind the girth where it should have been. There is an indentation in the flesh there to accommodate the horse's lungs and my leg was safely in this gap, not really being crushed by the weight of the horse but instead shielded by its anatomy.

Proper equitation is saving my leg. I really couldn't believe that. It's not just for show or function, it's for safety too.

After what seemed like minutes Mo finally decided to get up, scrambling his front legs wide to get a grip so he could hurl his neck forward, and in doing so bring his hind legs underneath him enough to push off and stand upright. As soon as he lifted his shoulders up, I began shaking my foot wildly, not enough to kick him but enough to get my foot free. I was able to do so before he even took a wobbly step forward. Crisis averted.

As I stood up, Tom walked over to me. Not in a panic, but of concern and a desire to help. He didn't help me up though, he just waited to be told what to do, to be asked. Chivalrous as he was, he let me stand on my own two feet, literally, and I appreciated him for that.

But as soon as I went to stand up, I realized I couldn't put a ton of weight on my foot, and almost buckled to the ground. Without being asked Tom grabbed me by the arm and held me up.

"Thanks," I said and looked up at him with a weak smile and a lot of gratitude. This might go somewhere.

He helped me hobble out of the arena, as I held one foot up and grabbed my horse's reins. Hurt foot or not, he still needed to be taken care of.

Tom helped me untack, and as he did my foot swelled to the point that it was uncomfortable to be in a boot. I took the boot off, and to my surprise my foot hurt a lot less. After taking a moment to palpate my foot and try putting weight in various spots, I figured it wasn't broken, just bruised badly on the arch where the caught stirrup had pressed into it while stuck under the horse.

I couldn't leave Mo in the stall though. He needed to be washed down, rubbed down with some liniment to soothe his muscles, and walked to prevent soreness. He took a pretty good fall, and I didn't want him to be sore because of it. So, shoeless and hobbling we went to the wash rack. Tom was amused at my one boot attire and tagged along. After watching me hobble for a bit, walking Mo around on the gravel parking lot, he offered his foot and his arm.
I looked at him, a little confused. I didn't understand the gesture, did he want me to dance?

"Walk on my foot" he said matter-of-factly, like it was no trouble at all and the easiest thing in the world.

"Walk...on your foot?" that seemed awful cumbersome, and like it would hurt him.

"Yeah" he smiled, a genuine smile that lit up at the eyes.

"Won't it hurt you?" I asked, I don't think I would want anyone to walk on my foot.

"Nope." He stuck his boot out again, inviting me to step on it.

So, I put my sock, damp from hosing off Mo, on his boot and looped my arm on the same side through his. With my other boot on the ground and my other hand holding Mo, I hobbled around that parking lot, walking on his foot, for the better part of a half hour.

If there was a way to make me fall in love, this was it. An unprompted, unasked and unforced selfless act. He was just there, offering the thing he had, himself, to me. He just wanted me to be more comfortable, even at his own expense. He lent me his leg, his foot, so I could do what I needed to do, take care of my horse. He didn't rush me, and he didn't ask for a break. He literally was a shoulder to lean on. And to think, before, I didn't even like him! No one had ever treated me so well. No one had ever cared that much; in the most complete way I had ever felt. He didn't judge me, he didn't make me feel bad about the fall, or the fact that I couldn't stop.

The purest human I had ever met, with a servant's heart offered me his foot. A horse gives you wings, and makes your heart soar, but a person can hold your heart close to theirs and make it feel safe.

-Adult Reflections-

I returned to that arena pretty close to when I wrote this story down for the first time. It was fifteen years later, and there was a gated chute this time.
Progress.

It wasn't bravery that I needed, although you can't control every show producer or facility and need to be up for anything. I was right, there was a glaring safety hazard that needed to be addressed. People just didn't because it was too much work and nothing bad had happened yet. I guess someone must have gotten in a real wreck to get the gates put up eventually.

I think in the western riding world there is a lot of pressure to be tough and just roll with anything. I think those are valuable traits, but there's a time and a place for both. There are, after all, unavoidable things and avoidable things. Unavoidable is having to be very good and fast at stopping quick and watching out for other people as you do. This is present at every barrel racing event.

Avoidable is creating a situation designed to fail, and then being mad when people do fail because they are not "tough enough."

Was my lack of control the primary reason for the wreck? Absolutely.

But lots of people get out of control, lots of people are learning.

This is not the Oregon trail; we don't need to be the strongest to survive a horse show. Some basic measures can go a long way in helping to keep people safer, although we can never eliminate all risk.

As an adult, I advocate for my safety and the safety of others under my direction. If I don't like facility's set up or policies, I don't go there.

In terms of the riding, any time you do a one rein stop at high speed as I did, you risk a fall. This method is most effective in the first few moments of a bolt or a spook, not a way to slow down at high speed. Obviously, it can work, but you risk having your horse slip out from under you, and pancake on the ground like mine did. I knew the risk and did it anyway, and the situation being what it was, I still think it was the right decision. The solution was to address the root of the problem, lack of stopping from a run, before it got to the point that I had to make a decision like that.

If your horse falls and you know you are going down with them, kick your feet out before you hit, so you can get free as soon as they get up.

Lastly, marry someone who lets you walk around on their foot. I did.

Alex Tyson

One More Before You Go

This last story I feel encompasses the journey that I was on as a young rider, and the type of person I emerged as after all these incidents.

I wanted to do things right, but I really didn't understand the nuances of everything. Some things, like the train tracks, were just things that happened. Others, like making the judge laugh, and the failure to stop with Mo, were a part of growth and learning.

The more you ride, the more risk you take, and the more likely something will go wrong at some point.
I would even put some of the Pepper stories into this category. Owning a horse is a much different than leasing a horse or riding lesson horses. There is so, so, so much to learn, and as you learn more, you will discover so much of what you still don't know.

But most of the stories, I knew better, at least theoretically, but I went on anyway.

I think I continued on because I didn't want to believe it was true…it was inconvenient at the time…other people were doing it…other people didn't seem worried about it…and the most juvenile of all: this doesn't apply to me because I am an advanced rider. Please. I was advanced in terms of technical skill and riding ability, but part of what makes an advanced rider is doing what needs to be done, regardless of what other people are doing or the potential damage to your own ego. An advanced rider does what is best for the horse, and is mindful of possible situations that might go "sideways."

Part of how you get there is how I did, live and learn, but I think it would be in the horse's best interest if I had listened a bit more and did a little less.

The crazy thing was that there were people who did far crazier things around me and didn't get hurt, furthering my youthful exploration of "is this *really* dangerous?" In many ways I was the rule follower among my peers, I just had lapses in judgment that resulted in some wild stories. Sure, there are folks with wilder stories, and I am not out to be the most outrageous. I just want to share the stupid things I did and how I learned from them. Maybe I got a laugh, maybe I made someone think a bit more about a decision they were about to make. There were tons of things I didn't do because I heard a story that scared me out of it. Stories inspire as well; I didn't die, so there is a chance you won't as well on your own adventures (but please be careful).

This final story, was not only a turning point in my riding career, but it was a turning point for me as a person. Only in looking back can I really see that I was able to balance stubborn recklessness with a bit of wisdom which is the blueprint for nearly everything I do today.

Alex Tyson

Eventually

"He will stop you know…" The Cowboy said to me in a huge open field that was close to a mile around the whole perimeter.

"Eventually…" He finished with a chuckle as his voice trailed off to survey the expanse of land before him. It was huge, it was hard to believe it was a pasture.

I knew he was right, but it didn't make this any easier. Mo just would not stop after a barrel run. I had almost fallen off by playing chicken with a fence a few times, and I had literally sideswiped a few riders by smashing Mo into the side of them, the horse's bellies and the rider's legs scraping past each other. I had gotten a reputation as *that poor girl who can't stop her horse.*

It was absurd though, because in the arena I could ride Mo on a loose rein at the walk, trot and canter and just sit down to slam to a halt. I had even ridden him bridle-less. He stopped perfectly off of my seat, and he was super soft in the mouth. He knew how to break at the poll and round up, he could be guided with fingertip ease. He didn't get overly excited when he ran, he just would not come back to me at a run. I had been trying now for almost a year, and the last big show of the season, the NBHA State Finals, was closing in. Even after close to twenty shows that season, my brakes were non- existent. It got to the point where people didn't want to be in the arena with me and would find a way to leave, so I wouldn't hit them as I came, quite literally, screaming in.

"You just have to sit back more and pull!" The Cowboy said, a little exasperated, repeating it for the hundredth time.

"He knows you don't mean business, and he is taking advantage."

I hung my head a little and nodded. No one else seemed to have this problem. Not like this.

I was sitting back as hard as I could, pushing my feet forward, bracing on them and sending my shoulders behind the saddle, I pulled on the reins, took and gave the reins, see-sawed the reins, anything and everything, but nothing worked. Mo even had a gag bit with a twisted mouthpiece — one of the strongest bits out there--which made no difference. I knew, and so did everyone else including The Cowboy, that I was the problem.

I could also tell that The Cowboy was losing faith in me. He once treated me like a child prodigy, his adopted daughter, riding colts and breaking horses, quite a few of them. He toted me around with pride, beaming that I was under his tutelage, happy that he had found a star to carry on his legacy. Mo was supposed to further that legacy-the talented kid was now on the talented horse. I didn't live up to expectations, I am sure. I was stuck, and I certainly wasn't going faster. His star wasn't shinning, and I felt him move onto the next rising star and focus more of his attention there.

That said, he was still here. He still was trying to help me, albeit saying the same thing over and over and growing further away by the day, but he was still here.
It sounds silly to have such an emotional attachment to one's horse trainer, but when your own parental figure is, well, not, then you latch on to what you have. Not having any children (at least not that I knew of) I think The Cowboy relished his role for awhile, but didn't understand the complexities of it himself. It wasn't perfect, but it was what I had, and I felt it slipping away.

That day he was on his own horse with me. He wanted to get his young colts used to galloping more; wind sprints he called them. I ran after him and I got my usual result: no brakes, and it took what would have been the length of two arenas to stop.

    The Cowboy just shook his head as I walked back over to him, unsuccessful yet again. Maybe I don't have what it takes to ride these kinds of horses.

    "I guess keep doing it till you figure it out. You'll get sick of it eventually, one day you'll have enough and finally get that sucker to stop." He turned away as he said this, walking his horse the long path back to the barn. I am glad he did because he missed a little tear budding in my eye. He was giving up on me.

    I turned over what The Cowboy said every day. I watched videos of myself running, I watched videos of other people running, and I just could not figure out what I was doing wrong. I wasn't squeezing him, I definitely was sitting back, and I definitely was pulling back. My hands were not too low or too high. I looked tense, yes, and I didn't look like I believed he would stop. But, how can you believe something is going to happen when it never has? There must be something wrong with me, something I can't figure out.

    Maybe I am just not cut out for this. Maybe I can't ride how I need to. Maybe I am not that good at riding, period. That was a terrifying thought. Riding was the only thing in the world I was good at. It was my rock and my safe space in this world. Here I could be good at something, I had friends, I had a family. But all of that would go away if I couldn't ride how I needed to. You had to ride with the big boys to stay in their club.

    Weeks and many galloping sessions went by with essentially no improvement. The only thing I can say is I did feel better in the gallop itself, but that didn't really translate to stopping. Stopping was the problem, not galloping. I tried to hulk myself out more, I didn't like the idea of pulling so much on a horse but this seemed to be what was required. It didn't sit well with me, but I persisted.

Then, one day, racking my brain for something, anything that would be of use to me, I thought of one of my favorite horse movies: *Seabiscuit*.

Seabiscuit is a movie about the famous racehorse, an underdog who won a lot of races during the Great Depression. In the last scene, at the end of the race, the jockey stands in the stirrups, shifting his weight back and elevating his shoulders, from his incredibly bent galloping position. He doesn't pull when he does, he just lets up and coasts for a bit, chest out, hovering, a transition period. Then he starts to pull the reins and eventually an outrider will come and get him, pulling up the racing animal much like Maggie pulled up Sampson for me.

That might be it! Mo used to race on the track. A sprint track, not the same distance as *Seabiscuit*, but a track nonetheless. Pulling at this speed just makes him go faster, obviously, even though he accepts bit contact going slower. What if, oh, what if, I sit back without pulling, and then lightly ask?

The more I thought about it, the more I thought it might work. There was just one problem with my logic: The Cowboy had not suggested this. In fact, he and everyone else I talked to insisted on just the opposite. Sit back more, pull harder, be tougher. He was the person I respected most; he'd always had the answers before-so why not now?

Even so, I just knew in my gut that his advice wasn't working.

I had to try this, even if I was the only one who thought it would work. It wasn't just some stupid idea; it had some teeth to it. There was evidence for it. I had to try.

I needed to be all alone just in case this went awry, and I didn't want to tell The Cowboy about my idea. If he had a fault that I could see, it was that he was a proud man, and wanted people to respect and love him. The idea of doing something different than how he would do it would have greatly offended him.

I had been around horses long enough now to know that there are different theories and modes of doing things. People often times got into trouble when they weren't solid in what they knew, and cherry-picked things from opposing philosophies, thoroughly confusing them and their horses. You're meant to trust the process of your "master" and learn all he had to learn, the way they wanted you to learn it. Going rogue was considered reckless and rebellious, indicative of someone who had a disdain for the rules and learning in general; a person doomed to fail.

At the same time, I had also heard lots of stories of people who come up with a new way of training horses, even when everyone around them was doing the opposite. I knew quite a bit about Monty Roberts, a man who tamed a Mustang in the wild named Shy Boy. I had read about him and seen some of his demos-he was communicating through body language, the horse's language. I had even learned some of the technique he taught in the round pen from a book and I was amazed that the horse would follow me around afterward, no ropes, licking and chewing, calm and with me, just like the book said they would.

I had a lot of success with my young horses using these techniques, although I knew I had definitely not mastered them. The Cowboy had not taught me these things, but didn't stop me from doing it either. But still, it was something different, I could tell it was a step farther than The Cowboy was willing to go.

There were lots of people who had built on these ideas, the Natural Horsemanship movement, some called it. I had seen lots of folks toting this line of thinking at horse expos that I had been to, and I was fascinated by them. A lot of these folks didn't like the way things were, so they made their own way. How does one determine where the line is? How long do you have to do something before you can change? Who allows you to?

I didn't have those answers, but I had to give my wild idea a try. I had a terrifying hunch that I was right, but I knew for certain that, If I didn't figure this out, it wasn't going to happen.

Resolved, off to the field we went.

I scouted out all my routes. I knew right where I was going to send him, where I was going to coast, and where I needed to pull up. Or try to, at least. I had almost a mile to get it right, and I was committed to *not* sawing his face off. It wasn't working anyway; I would do something new.

I called Mo "the freight train" because he felt like a massive train chugging along with all the weight and power in the back pushing forward, not likely to slow down anytime soon. This horse was the pinnacle of athleticism, his short back, and strong, sloping hindquarters, made him a sprinting and turning machine. I feared him but needed to accept in my heart that we were not going to stop soon.

I had to believe if I thought ahead, if I planned and breathed, if I acted like a jockey, that he would feel me and come back.

Sounds crazy. Pull less on the horse that doesn't stop. I also knew I needed to really send him this time. Show him that I would stay with him. I had to tell him to run faster, faster than I ever had before. I couldn't hold back.
I didn't have much to lose, and in a lot of ways it felt like a doomed mission.

If I couldn't do this, there wasn't much else to do. Even if I pushed it too far and perished trying to do this, well, so be it. This was all I could be, and if can't be it, there isn't much point to anything else.

I'll go out swinging, or rather running, if that is what it takes.

With that I hardened my eyes, took a deep breath, and sprung up out of the saddle, forward and committed. I sent my freight train down the lane to nowhere. With nothing, nothing to lose.

In this way, I found freedom.

I sent that horse faster than I have ever run before. My heart and his heart were one, pumping out all of my frustration into a blazing surge that felt like it would go upward, eventually, towards the heavens.
Tears flew from my eyes as the wind yanked them out, dirt and grass spraying everywhere, a storm swirling beneath those hooves. A storm playing out in my chest. We were running, but it many ways it seemed like we were screaming.
    Screaming at what could be but wasn't.
    Screaming at our own misunderstandings.
    Screaming because we were young and restless.
    Screaming into the wind, where no one could hear us.
    The ground lapped up beneath us as we charged on, madmen towards our own destruction, consumed by an untenable fire.
    The birds sang and the world turned, perhaps someone died and someone was born; but I was running.
Hope scorched me as I blazed ahead, scraping away at my being, burning me alive. burning up with all the hopes of a girl who tried her best and still it's not enough.
    It is never enough.
    I might have screamed but I couldn't have heard myself even if I did, the hurried breathing of Mo sucking in gallons of air drowning out any other sound. The rock of that gallop pulled the rage out of my chest, step by step, halfway around the field now but deep within ourselves, stride by stride we understood now what the meaning of life was, and how it felt to be here, balanced on the edge of it.

Rage waned, as if put out by God himself, and the fire began to cool.

Suddenly I was no longer angry, and Mo no longer frustrated, pulling me along. I felt this feeling of settling, as if galloping was no longer exciting, we were no longer pushing the limits, pushing towards death. Now, we were just galloping, just a pace one traveled. I felt Mo cool it, no longer a freight train, just carrying on because I asked him to. The rage was gone.

While still blazing fast, and imperceptible to anyone who would have seen, we were no longer screaming. It was more of a hum. A hum that knew the melody.

Something had changed.

It was time.

I stopped asking Mo to run, but I stayed in my galloping position. I then slowly lifted my shoulders up and pushed my feet a little forward, and my weight a little back. I just made the balance change and hovered, right between Go and Whoa and waited.

And three strides later I felt it.

The recoil, the coming back to me. A chorus of angels sang in my head, It had worked!

It was enough.

It was only then that I sat myself down, bumpy as galloping is and relaxed my body, willing Mo to come back to me.

It only took another eight strides to come back to a nice, brisk trot, in control and calm.

It was the easiest thing on Earth. It was like we had done it 1,000 times instead of one.

I threw myself onto Mo's neck as we reached the walk and wrapped my arms under it, holding tight to him, to this moment, to possibilities.

I sobbed and sobbed into Mo's neck with an elation that could rival no other Earthly thing.

I had done it; I had overcome. I had figured it out.

I had become the rider that Mo needed me to be. I could stop him. I had accomplished the thing I had struggled with the most, but I did it alone. I didn't do what people said, but what I knew was right. What worked was kinder to the horse and required more of me. Not so much physically, but mentally.

I loved The Cowboy, but he had been wrong. I now had more questions than answers.

New possibilities were a foot, there was another world out there, another way to solve some of these problems, and I had just scratched the surface.

Still, as I walked Mo out, I wrestled with myself the whole way back. Conflicting feelings of jubilation, guilt, astonishment, disbelief, and pride.

I was brave but I wasn't stupid. I was soft but I wasn't weak. I was strong, but I didn't overpower.

And the grace, the grace of this horse to let me figure this out. So earnest, so willing to try, yet again, when there was no evidence that it would be successful.

Mo did what I couldn't: he believed me when there wasn't any reason to.

We, truly, don't deserve horses.

~Adult Reflections~

Nuance is so, so difficult, and the details of a particular situation matter.

The root problem here was tension. My tension.

Nothing, in my experience, is harder to fix.

The Cowboy had the right idea by getting me to gallop more, outside of a show scenario, and stopping the horse where it didn't really matter how long it took to stop. This would have been the worst thing to do if the problem was the horse stopping, but the problem was me stopping the horse.

Whether he either couldn't explain himself properly or didn't recognize the root of the problem I will never know. I do know that teaching other people is HARD, and harder still when dealing with a complex problem at a high rate of speed.

I am not angry at him. I think he was trying to help me the best that he knew how and told me what had worked for him and others. What is important in this story is not so much about him, but the growth I made for myself. I learned countless lessons over the years from many runaway horses, and I formulated a plan based around that knowledge, even if no one else saw what I saw.

That, really, is how you make a horseman: balance and riding technique, experience, knowledge from lessons learned, and an action plan based on those things.

Mo was no longer a runaway horse.

I had finally learned.

Many Runaway Horses

Afterward

I grew up, and made a career with horses.

I earned a CHA (Certified Horseman's Association) riding instructor certification.

I run a horseback riding school and have taught hundreds of people to ride a horse from scratch.

I have taken at least 200 people to their first horse show, and coached many on to rated-show success.

I have trained several #1 National High Point horses and youth riders in Working Equitation.

I have had Top 3 and Top 5 finishes at the Thoroughbred Makeover, a major national retraining competition that retrains recently off-the-track Thoroughbred horses into new careers.

I have broken feral horses, and BLM Mustangs.

I have won a bridle-less freestyle.

My point? I went on to do all this, despite once being young and dumb. Everyone starts out as one or both of these. Slowly, as the stories show, I moved on from clueless to making bad choices thinking I knew better to making better choices. While I was exceptionally advanced for my age, I embodied what is reality for a lot of kids: moments of brilliance surrounded by adolescent chaos. However, I was truly motivated by my "dads" and they are the reason I was able to piece together the best version of my teen self. Eventually, it turned into something I could be proud of.

I also had hardly any money to do all of this. My mom, who allowed me to have a horse, later had to file for bankruptcy. We didn't really have enough money to be doing horses, but, through a mother's love, we did it anyway. At one point we even cashed out some college savings so I could go to horse shows.

There is almost always help if you are willing to put the time and effort in to learn. And the work you put in may not be reciprocal to what is given. But really, it is. Any opportunity to learn is like gold. Read books, watch others' lessons, save up for your own lessons. Learn, learn, learn. You can always learn.

The grace of horses will always amaze me. How they let us begin anew. How they forgive.

I hope these stories made you laugh, made you think, and made you appreciate God's most noble creature, the horse.

I hope they inspire you to become the rider that your horse deserves.

I hope they are a cautionary tales of what can happen, and maybe how not to do it.

I hope you go on your own horse adventures. They will never free from perils, but maybe, just maybe, you almost die and learn.

Alex Tyson

Riding Through it Glossary

For quick reference, here is a general guide to how to ride some of the things I was riding. To ride it you have to be an excellent rider, to correct it, better still. Always seek professional help if you have to deal with something like this:
Bolting: this usually happens as the result of something scary. The good old one-rein-stop is your friend here. But you must react precisely. Get stiff too early in anticipation and you make it worse. Wait too long to run their nose in the wall and you make it a lot harder to be successful. It has to been done in the first stride or two.
Shying: This is where the horse is afraid of a usually stationary object or a quick movement. You use the one-rein stop again, but in the direction of the scary thing, having them stand and face it. Walking up to it and letting them sniff is usually next. You have to be pretty oriented to which direction they are spooking; both to stay on, and to correct the spook.
Bucking: my least favorite of all. Bucking happens most often at the canter. Yank their head up to keep it from getting in between their legs and kick them forward, moving out of the buck. There are different levels of buck, a buck where their back legs are over their head you just need to stay on, stop it and regroup.
Rearing: a refusal to go forward or a refusal to stand. Q would do it typically when asked her to go forward after she spooked at something. When going up all one can do is ride the rear, grabbing the neck, NOT pulling back on the reins, and hinging your body forward with the horse, almost laying on their neck. If you are very experienced and have expert timing, going down from the rear you could start to open your hand and get their feet moving in a circle, riding pretty

aggressively until that circle turned into forward. Always forward.

About the Author:

Alex Tyson is a C.H.A. Certified riding instructor, trainer, and clinician in Southeast MI. Alex began riding and competing in hunter/jumper style events in Michigan, and eventually switched to barrel racing, where she was able to qualify and compete at the 2010 NBHA Youth World Championships.

At nineteen, Alex completed the Ken McNabb horse training apprenticeship program and went on to form her own horseback riding school.

Alex has gentled and trained BLM Mustangs, off the track Thoroughbreds, and enjoys training the more "difficult" ones.

A fan of training competitions, Alex had top finishes at the 2021 Thoroughbred Mega Makeover in Lexington, Kentucky.

Alex's students have been ranked #1 in several National Youth High Point spots for Working Equitation.
Alex herself has won many Working Equitation competitions, including the 2022 Cross Nations Cup, Intermediate A Division, in Missoula, MT.

When not riding horses (which isn't often) Alex enjoys hiking, traveling, and fueling her excessive coffee addiction.

Made in the USA
Monee, IL
21 January 2023

25531714R00142